PSE North Country Closeouts 10-11-03

The Bean Book

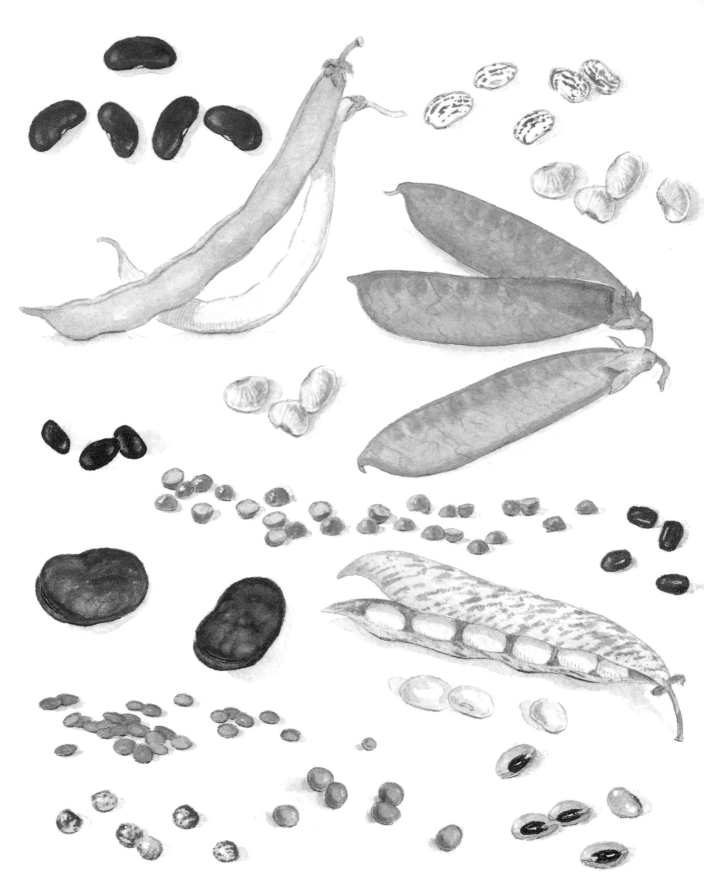

The Bean Book

Roy F. Guste, Jr.

Illustrations by Roger Yepsen

W. W. Norton & Company

NEW YORK | LONDON

TO THE MATASSAS FOR FOOD,
FRANK BRUNO FOR SHELTER, AND
CHRISSY FOR ENCOURAGEMENT.

Copyright © 2001 by Roy F. Guste, Jr.

The text of this book is composed in ITC Galliard with the display set in Arrus BT
Book design and composition by John Bernstein
Illustrations by Roger Yepsen
Printed in Singapore

Library of Congress Cataloging-in-Publication Data

Guste, Roy F.
      The bean book / Roy F. Guste, Jr.

           p.   cm.
      Includes index.
      ISBN 0-393-04926-4

1. Cookery (Beans) 1. Title

TX803.B4 G87 2000
641.6'565 – dc21   00-041121

W.W. Norton & Company, Inc., 500 Fifth Avenue, New York, NY 10110
www.wwnorton.com

W.W. Norton & Company Ltd., 10 Coptic Street, London WC1A 1PU

1 2 3 4 5 6 7 8 9 0

Contents

Introduction

Humans have always eaten beans, first as hunter/gatherers, then as cultivators. Beans were among the first plants cultivated. There is archaeological evidence of bean cultivation in Asia and South and Central America as early as seven thousand years ago. Bean plants have been used at all stages of their development. Leaves were used as green vegetables; as were the immature pods; fresh beans were removed from the pods and eaten. Beans that were dried in the pod, on the trailing vine or bush of the bean plant, were stored for future use. These dried beans were often used to grow sprouts for raw consumption, or they were cooked. And some of the dried beans were planted again. Finally, in some early cultures beans were used as currency.

Most of the beans which we know in the United States belong to the same family, Phaseolus vulgaris. They originated in South and Central America, and were brought to North America by trading Indians before the arrival of the Europeans.

The aboriginal tribes of the Americas had developed a sophisticated method of agriculture which included a trio of important food plants: maize (corn), beans, and squash. The corn was planted at the center of the group with the beans planted around it, and the squash around the beans. The corn would grow and develop while giving the trailing bean vines a stake on which to climb. The squash leaves would attract insects away from the corn and beans without damage to the squash. The three plants actually fertilized one another by returning essential elements to the soil, especially nitrogen from the bean plants.

One of the many great losses resulting from the European "discovery" of the Americas is that the proven symbiotic relationship between soil and plants was given up. European methods of row farming stripped the earth of nutrients and top soil.

This book concerns itself with beans, peas, and lentils (sometimes called pulses). To understand the proper relationship of particular pulses to individual cuisines of the world it is necessary to place each bean, pea, or lentil in its distinct location of origin. It is also useful to know which other food plants, recognizable to Americans, originated in these locations. The following, which interests me greatly as a food historian, is a general list of origins of many of the world's foods. I have organized the placement of origin by beginning with the Americas and moving eastward around the world.

. . . .

North America

— No pulses (beans, peas, and lentils) originated here, but the red bean, runner bean (Phaseolus vulgaris) was already disseminated here from Mesoamerica by the time of European exploration.

Other foods

— Jerusalem artichoke or topinambour (tuber)
— Sunflower (edible seeds and oil)
— Strawberry, minor grape varieties, cranberry (fruits)
— Pecans (nuts)
— Tobacco (stimulant)

Mesoamerica

— beans (Phaseolus vulgaris), red, white, black, pinto, green: all common beans
— maize (corn)

— sweet potato, cassava, jícama (roots and tubers)
— cotton (oil and fiber)
— papaya, avocado, guava, prickly pear (fruits)
— capsicum peppers, squash, tomato (vegetables)
— vanilla (spice)
— cacao (stimulant)

South America

— common beans (Phaseolus vulgaris)
— jack bean (legume)
— lupin (legume)
— potato, cassava, jícama, arracacha, achira, oca, anu, yacon, ullucru, mashua, unchuc
— peanut (seed legume and oil)
— cotton (oil)
— cashew, Brazil nut (nuts)

— pineapple, guava, guanabana, cherimoya (mirliton, vegetable pear), papaya, avocado (fruits)

— capsicum peppers, squash (vegetables)

— cacao, mate (stimulants)

Africa

— black-eyed pea — Africa and India — (cowpea, southern pea), Bambara groundnut, hyacinth bean, Kersting's groundnut (legumes)

— African rice, pearl millet, sorghum, fonio, tef (cereals)

— oil palm, castor bean (oils)

— watermelon, melons, baobab (fruits)

— okra (vegetable)

— sesame (seeds and oil)

— coffee (stimulant)

Southeast Asia

— pigeon pea, jack bean, winged bean, moth bean, rice bean (legumes)

— Asian rice (cereal)

— coconut (meat and oil)

— yam, taro, arrowroot (roots and tubers)

— orange, tangerine, lime, grapefruit, banana, breadfruit, mango (fruits)

— cucumber, plantain (vegetables)

— pepper (black pepper), nutmeg (spices)

— coconut (meat and oil)

Near East

— pea, lentil, chickpea (garbanzo), lupines (legumes)

— turnip, carrot, radish (roots and tubers)

— fig, date palm, grape, apple, pear, plum (fruits)

— almond, walnut (nuts)

— olives (meat and oil)

— rapeseed, safflower, flax (oils)

— onion, lettuce (vegetable)

— saffron, parsley, coriander (spice, herb)

— poppy, digitalis, belladonna, licorice (stimulants)

China

— soybean, adzuki bean (legumes)

— Asian rice, prose, foxtail millet (cereals)

— turnip, yams (roots and tubers)

— peach, apricot, quince, persimmon, litchi (fruits)

— Chinese hickory, chestnut (nuts)

— Chinese cabbage (vegetable)

— ginger (spice)

— rapeseed (oil)

— tea, ginseng, camphor (stimulants)

Beans as medicine

The many people suffering from clogged arteries, alcoholism, and sleep disorders may someday depend on the benefits that some legumes can provide.

Black beans and soybeans are rich sources of genistein, which is being studied for use in lowering the risk of breast and prostate cancers as well as heart disease. It also is thought to fight leukemia. Soybeans also contain high levels of daidzein, which the Chinese have long used as an herbal medicine and to cut the craving for alcohol.

The winged bean contains high levels of proteins called lectins. Medical researchers use lectins as diagnostic tools because they bind to certain blood cells in the body. This makes them valuable in vaccine research, especially in the direction of edible vaccines. Winged beans also contain erucic acid, an anti-tumor medication, as well as polyunsaturated fatty acids that can be used to treat acne and eczema.

The velvet bean, contains bufotenine, a cholinesterase inhibitor, and serotonin, a brain neurotransmitter, which may aid learning, sleep, and the control of moods.

Beans are medicine for the earth because they help fix nitrogen in the soil.

Beans as starch dishes

We should all try to reconsider our use of beans and think of them in a way that they are thought of in many countries other than the United States.

Beans should become imprinted in our culinary repertoire as replacement for less nutritional starches, a food that can be used regularly in place of other less beneficial starches: white rice, potatoes, barley, grits, couscous, polenta, and pasta.

Beans are high in fiber and protein when compared to other starches that have little or no fiber and protein. For example, when you prepare a roast or a baked chicken, use beans as your side starch and spoon the gravy over the beans just as you would on rice or mashed potatoes. Mash the beans as you would potatoes if you like. Beans are more filling because of the fiber content; they require more work, more calories from your body to digest so you actually use more of the bean calories you are eating to digest than you would other starches.

Their carbohydrates are more complex and leave your body with less of the "sugar" drop that you get from other starches. Your craving for sweets and desserts after dinner will be reduced. They help reduce cholesterol in your system, something which no other starch can claim. Just as your craving for sweets can be reduced, so can your craving for alcohol. Beans improve sleep patterns.

The following is a comparison of nutritional values of white rice, mashed potatoes, and pasta to black beans:

. . . .

Measure = 1 cup cooked of each (no added salt or fat)

	black bean		white rice		mashed potato		pasta	
Calories	227		266		203.6		197.4	
Protein	15.3	g	2.5	g	4.4	g	6.7	g
Carbohydrates	40.8	g	57.8	g	47.0	g	39.6	g
Dietary Fiber	15	g	1.1	g	4.2	g	2.1	g
Fat	.9	g	.6	g	.2	g	.9	g
Cholesterol	0	mg	0	mg	0	mg	0	mg
Sodium	1.7	mg	2	mg	9.4	mg	1.4	mg

Percent of Calories				
Protein	26%	9%	8%	14%
Carbohydrates	70%	89%	91%	82%
Fat	4%	2%	1%	4%

The two areas that are most impressive are protein and fiber, both necessary and beneficial to our diet. Beans also provide the vegetarian and vegan with the protein lacking in most vegetable products.

One cup of black beans is a full meal; a cup of the others is not. I say this because one cup of black beans will fill you up; the others will not, at least not for me.

A rather important note about beans in relationship to developing countries is that beans will produce twenty-five times as much protein on an acre of land as meat protein production from animal pasturing.

Preparing beans for cooking

Rinsing and sorting

The first step to preparing beans for cooking is to rinse and sort them. This is an important first step because the process removes any dust or dirt that may still be attached to the beans. During this process it is necessary to sort out any pebbles or other particles from the beans, as well as sorting out any broken or floating beans. But to me, even more important than cleaning the beans, the rinsing and sorting process washes the olioglycerides from the outside skins of the beans. These olioglycerides are partly responsible for flatulence.

Soaking

Although beans can be cooked without soaking, it is far better to soak them before cooking. The reason for this is that dried beans require rehydration, or absorption of water, to cook evenly, without splitting in the cooking. If the beans split during the cooking they will become a mass rather than separate cooked beans. "Creamed" beans are a neophyte's answer to improperly cooked beans. Soaking also reduces the cooking time by at least half.

There is also a quick-soak method that simply requires that you simmer the washed, unsoaked beans for 2 or 3 minutes and leave to soak in the hot water for 1 hour. Then drain and proceed as for overnight soaked beans. Overnight soaked beans means that they are soaked for 6 or more hours. The term overnight is used because it is easier to leave beans soaking for their 6 hours or more overnight than to wait the 6 hours soaking time on the day you are cooking the beans. The term "soak" in this book refers to either way you prefer.

Beans will almost triple in size during soaking. Don't be shy with the water. Make sure that the beans have several inches of water covering them in your soaking container.

Don't use the soaking water as the cooking water. There will be more olioglycerides released into the water during the soaking.

Do I personally ever cook beans without soaking? Yes. When I decide to have beans without time to soak. The cooking takes twice as long, sometimes as long as 3 hours.

Water measure for cooking

The measure of water added to the beans should be at least three to four times the measure of beans. A pound of dried beans is 2 cups: the water measure should be 6 to 8 cups.

Water can always be added during the cooking so simply keep the beans covered by the liquid as they cook. Excess liquid can be simmered off — reduced — when the beans are cooked.

Cooking beans

The most common cooking method for beans is boiling, or simmering. After the beans are rinsed and sorted, and soaked, transfer them to a pot with three or four times the water. Simmer for about 1 hour. Test the beans. The use of the beans — soup, entree, salads, puree and the firmness or tenderness desired — will determine the actual cooking time. Soaked beans can sometimes take only 1 hour to cook so test for tenderness as you cook. The size of the bean also affects the cooking time. A small red bean may take only an hour and a large kidney bean might take an hour and a half or more.

Methods of testing the tenderness of the bean are pressing a bean against the inside of the pot with a wooden spoon to mash it, or cooling a bean and placing it on your tongue and pressing it against the roof of your mouth to mash it. If the mashed bean reveals a still whitish center, it needs more cooking.

Salting the beans

Don't salt the beans until they reach the tenderness the recipe requires. Salting the beans before they tenderize will harden the beans and cause them to take more time to tenderize. Don't add any acidic products like vinegar, lemon, or tomatoes to the beans before they are tender. They will also cause the beans to harden and take longer to tenderize. Don't cook the beans in stock or broth until they are tender. The salt and protein in the stock will cause the beans to take longer to cook. Cook until tender in plain water.

I generally use 2 teaspoons of salt to a pound of cooked beans to start. Then I add more if that is not enough. If you use salty meats or additives to the beans to complete the recipe, use less salt to start. Remember that each individual can always add salt at the table.

Completing the recipe

Once the beans are tender, then you can add salt, other flavorants, and the additional ingredients of the recipe.

Thickening the liquid

The proper way to thicken the liquid is to mash some of the beans against the inside of the pot, stirring those in, until you have reached the texture you want in the liquid. This makes the liquid a sauce or gravy of the beans themselves and allows a better coating over rice or other foods. Or you can simmer the beans longer, uncovered.

The following chart lists suggested time information for soaking and cooking dried legumes, pulses (after soaking). These times will vary.

. . . .

Beans	Soaking Hours	Cooking Hours
aduki, adzuki	6–8	1
anasazi	6–8	1
black, turtle	6–8	1
brown	6–8	1
cannellini, white kidney	6–8	1
cranberry	6–8	1
great Northern (*white*)	6–8	1
navy (*white*)	6–8	1
pink, calico, red Mexican	6–8	1
pinto	6–8	1
red kidney beans	6–8	1
small red beans (*colorados*)	6–8	1

Other beans	Soaking Hours	Cooking Hours
fava, broad beans, ful nabed	12	3
small fava	12	3
limas, butter beans	6	1¼
young white	6	1¼
large white	6	1¼
tiny green limas	6	1
mung	6	¾
soybeans	12	3

Lentils	Soaking Hours	Cooking Hours
brown	0	¾
green	0	¾
red	0	¾
split red	0	¼

Peas	Soaking Hours	Cooking Hours
black-eyed, cowpea, China bean	0	1
chickpeas, garbanzo, gram	4	2
green	4	1
split green	0	½
pigeon peas	0	1
split yellow	0	½

This is a close approximation of the soaking and cooking times required to bring the legumes listed to the tender stage. Legumes that require soaking can be soaked overnight for convenience: They stop absorbing water after the times indicated and can be left to soak longer, without damage, if necessary.

Pressure cooking

Pressure cooking requires only about half of the normal cooking times. But the beans will require normal soaking.

Canned beans

Canned beans and legumes can be used in place of all recipes. This will enable the cook to forego all the rinsing, soaking, and cooking of the beans, making the process of cooking a bean recipe a last-minute effort when desired. Remember that canned beans are usually highly salted.

Cooking fresh legumes

Fresh tiny peas and small green beans can take as little as 2 minutes to cook. A larger pea or green bean can take up to 20 minutes. Test as you cook. Fresh soybeans, fava beans, and black-eyed peas will take only about 1 hour or less.

Green beans

Green beans, string beans, and snap beans are all the same basic bean (Phaseolus vulgaris). Choose beans that are fresh and plump, with a good fresh green color to them.

Unlike dried beans, green beans can be salted from the start of cooking without any discernable toughening.

To cook a pound of green beans bring enough water to cover to a boil with 2 teaspoons salt or more or less if you prefer. Simmer for 12 to 15 minutes, until just tender. Proceed with your recipe.

Fresh beans can also be steamed or microwaved in boiling water.

Unlike dried beans, fresh green beans can be cooked in salted stock or broth, or with other ingredients from the start.

All in all, pulses — beans, peas, and lentils — are the earth's most perfect plant food products.

Note on Nutritional Analyses

The nutritional analysis for each recipe is to be used — or not used — as you see fit. Because I am aware of what particular nutritional elements are important for my personal metabolism, I like to know what is in what I eat. If you are counting calories, fats, salt, protein, carbohydrates, fiber for a specific dietary regimen, the information is here for you.

I cook with two directions. First I follow classic recipes for full richness. Usually these are the dishes I serve to company and to myself on a special day. The lighter versions are dishes I would normally cook on a day-to-day basis. I see it as the best of both worlds.

The nutritional analysis for each recipe in this book is for a single serving or portion. If the recipe "serves, portions, or yields" for, say, 6 persons, then I have developed my "working" analyses using the full measure of recipe ingredients. Then I divided the analyses by the number of "servings, portions, or yield" to produce the per person analyses you see in this book. Although we can read the nutritional analysis on any food container, it is only with an understanding of entire daily nutritional needs does it make full sense. The following are the nutritional needs for most common groups: U.S. Female 25–50 years; U.S. Female 51+ years; U.S. Male 25–50 years; U.S. Male 51+ years. When you know what the daily nutritional needs are for your particular group, you will understand what part of those entire needs is met with each serving of each recipe.

Note on percents of calories

For some, this added information, not usually found in cookbooks, will be the most important. All dietary regimes, whether for weight loss, health improvement, illness recovery, or simply correct food consumption guidelines, should defer to the percentages and relationships of protein, carbohydrates, and fat in our food intake. In my own cooking I look for recipes that are low in calories with a low percentage of fat content. That's basically all I need to know. You will find that almost all of the lighter versions and many of the regular versions of the recipes in this book fall into this category: low-calorie with a low-fat percentage.

Too much information? I think not. My firm belief is that all dietary measures ultimately come down to what our specific group needs on a daily basis.

. . . .

Generic Profile Report
Recommended Daily Nutrients

BASIC COMPONENTS

	U.S. FEMALE		U.S. MALE	
	(25–50 yrs)	*(51+ yrs)*	*(25–50 yrs)*	*(51+ yrs)*
Calories	2092	1974	2945	2576
Protein	50 g	52 g	63 g	62 g
Carbohydrates	303 g	286 g	427 g	373 g
Dietary Fiber	21 g	20 g	29 g	26 g
Fat — Total	70 g	66 g	98 g	86 g
Saturated Fat	21 g	20 g	29 g	26 g
Mono Fat	26 g	24 g	36 g	31 g
Poly Fat	23 g	22 g	33 g	29 g
Cholesterol	300 mg	300 mg	300 mg	300 mg
Sodium	2400 mg	2400 mg	2400 mg	2400 mg

Green Beans

Phaseolus vulgaris

ORIGIN: CENTRAL AMERICA

The name *bean* covers a great many of the table vegetables that the world consumes as a substantial part of the human diet.

The common bean or true bean, as it is sometimes called, is a large family: Phaseolus vulgaris. This family contains most of the beans that we use on a regular basis.

The common bean is used in its early immature stage as a green bean, or string bean, then shelled while still not fully matured as a shell bean, and finally removed from the dried pod as the common dried bean, such as red bean, black bean, white bean, and all their numerous variations.

The common bean originated in Central America. It was cultivated there some six thousand years ago and widely disseminated in South and North America long before European exploration.

BOILED GREEN BEANS

Serves 6 as a side

1 ½ *pounds green beans*
1 *teaspoon salt*
¼ *teaspoon white pepper*

. . . .

1. Stem and string the beans if necessary and wash them.

2. Bring enough water to cover the beans to a rolling boil.

3. Plunge the beans into the boiling water, reduce heat somewhat, cover and simmer for about 12 minutes or to desired tenderness.

4. Drain.

5. Season to taste with salt and white pepper.

. . . .

Notes and Variations

Add a little lemon juice or a sprinkle of any kind of vinegar. Garnish with minced parsley, green onion, or a preferred fresh herb like basil, cilantro, or mint. Add several tablespoons of melted butter or olive oil for added richness. Remember that adding any fat adds calories.

NUTRITIONAL ANALYSIS

Calories:	34	
Protein:	2	g
Carbohydrates:	8	g
Dietary Fiber:	3	g
Fat:	.2	g
Cholesterol:	0	mg
Sodium:	358	mg

Percent of Calories

Protein:	18 %
Carbohydrates:	76 %
Fat:	6 %

STEAMED GREEN BEANS

Prepare the green beans as for the above recipe. The only real difference is that the beans are placed in a steamer, metal basket, or colander in a pot and held above water level. Garnish as above.

GREEN BEANS SAUTÉED WITH GARLIC, PARSLEY, AND LEMON *Serves 6 as a side*

1½ pounds green beans
8 tablespoons butter (1 stick)
6 cloves garlic, chopped
1 teaspoon salt
½ teaspoon white pepper
2 tablespoons lemon juice
¼ cup chopped parsley

. . . .

1. Boil the prepared green beans for about 8 minutes, until they begin to tenderize.

2. Melt the butter in a sauté pan or skillet and add the drained, boiled beans. Sauté for about 5 minutes and begin checking for tenderness. If tender, add the chopped garlic and continue sautéing for a minute more. Season to taste with salt and white pepper. Add the lemon juice and chopped parsley, cook for 1 minute more, and serve with the pan liquid poured over the beans.

Notes and Variations

Reduce the amount of butter if you feel
the fats are too high. Use olive oil
in place of butter for a different flavor.
Add rosemary and basil.

Calories:	177	
Protein:	2.5	g
Carbohydrates:	9.5	g
Dietary Fiber:	3.5	g
Fat:	16	g
Cholesterol:	41	mg
Sodium:	517	mg

Percent of Calories

Protein:	5%
Carbohydrates:	20%
Fat:	75%

HOT STRING BEAN SALAD WITH BACON DRESSING

Serves 6

2 pounds green beans, boiled or steamed
6 strips bacon, diced
¼ cup vinegar
1 ½ tablespoons sugar
½ teaspoon salt
1 teaspoon white pepper
3 green onions, chopped

1. Drain the beans and keep warm.

2. Sauté the diced bacon until crisp and carefully add the vinegar.

3. Add the sugar, salt, and pepper to the pan. Stir until all is hot and the sugar is completely dissolved.

4. Toss the hot beans with the hot bacon dressing. Adjust the seasonings if desired.

5. Garnish with the chopped green onions and serve.

NUTRITIONAL ANALYSIS

Calories:	317	
Protein:	3	g
Carbohydrates:	15	g
Dietary Fiber:	4.5	g
Fat:	28	g
Cholesterol:	28	mg
Sodium:	338	mg

Percent of Calories

Protein:	3%
Carbohydrates:	19%
Fat:	78%

GREEN BEANS WITH
NEW POTATOES AND HAM

Serves 6

4 *tablespoons butter*

½ *pound smoked ham, diced*

1 *medium onion, finely chopped*

12 *small new potatoes, scrubbed*

2 *cups water*

1 *pound green beans*

1 *teaspoon salt*

½ *teaspoon white pepper*

¼ *teaspoon cayenne pepper*

2 *tablespoons chopped parsley*

. . . .

1. In a saucepan, melt the butter and sauté the diced ham and onion for 3 minutes.

2. Add the potatoes and water. Cover and simmer for about 10 minutes, until the potatoes are just tender.

3. Add the green beans and season to taste with salt, white pepper, and cayenne. Cover and simmer for 5 to 8 minutes longer, until the beans are tender and the liquid is reduced.

4. If desired, adjust the seasonings and reduce the liquid further with the pan uncovered.

5. Fold in the chopped parsley and serve.

Notes and Variations

If you eliminate the butter and ham, the fats are reduced to less than 1 gram, the cholesterol to 0 milligrams, and the calories to 70. Carrots or turnips can be used in place of potatoes.

NUTRITIONAL ANALYSIS

Calories:	188	
Protein:	10.5	g
Carbohydrates:	15	g
Dietary Fiber:	4	g
Fat:	10	g
Cholesterol:	39	mg
Sodium:	979	mg

Percent of Calories

Protein:	22 %
Carbohydrates:	32 %
Fat:	46 %

CZECHOSLOVAKIAN FRESH GREEN BEAN AND POTATO SOUP

Serves 8

3 *tablespoons olive oil*

1 *large onion, finely chopped*

3 *large potatoes, scrubbed and diced*

2 *quarts chicken stock, or more if necessary*

1 *pound fresh green beans, stemmed and cut into ½-inch lengths*

1 *large tomato, skinned, seeded and chopped*

1 *teaspoon white pepper*

1 *tablespoon paprika*

2 *teaspoons salt*

1 *cup sour cream*

1. Heat the olive oil in a large saucepan and sauté the onion until just limp.

2. Add the diced potatoes and continue cooking, stirring, for about 5 minutes.

3. Add the chicken stock and bring to a simmer. Cover and continue simmering until the potatoes are very soft, about 30 minutes.

4. Using a whisk, beat the soft potato dice into the pot liquid to produce a homogeneous texture. Add more stock or water if the mixture becomes too thick.

5. Add the green beans, tomato, and season with white pepper, paprika, and salt. Cover and continue simmering for 15 to 20 minutes, until the beans are cooked but not too soft.

6. Remove from the heat, adjust the seasonings if desired, and whisk in the sour cream and serve.

. . . .

Notes and Variations

The chicken stock can be replaced with water, veal stock, or beef stock. I leave the skins on the potatoes for almost all dishes, even for mashed potatoes. I prefer the flecks of skin to add not only a more interesting look but a richer flavor — a more nutritious recipe. As always, when using stock in a recipe, be certain that the additions of salt and pepper are measured against the salt and pepper in the stock. This soup is like vichyssoise with beans.

. . . .

Lighter Version

Omit the olive oil and salt. Replace the stock with unsalted, nonfat broth, stock, or water. Replace the sour cream with nonfat sour cream. Add 1 teaspoon dried thyme to the paprika and stir in ¼ cup chopped fresh parsley to finish.

NUTRITIONAL ANALYSIS

	Regular		Lighter Version	
Calories:	264		134	
Protein:	9.5	g	4.5	g
Carbohydrates:	29	g	29	g
Dietary Fiber:	4.5	g	3.2	g
Fat:	13	g	<1	g
Cholesterol:	13	mg	0	mg
Sodium:	1335	mg	40	mg

Percent of Calories

Protein:	14%		13%	
Carbohydrates:	43%		84%	
Fat:	43%		2%	

Fresh Green Bean Salad   *Serves 4*

 1 *quart water, or enough to cover the beans*
 2 *teaspoons salt*
 1 *pound fresh young green beans, stringed*
 ¼ *cup olive oil*
 2 *tablespoons cider vinegar*
 1 *clove garlic, minced*
 1 *tablespoon chopped fresh cilantro leaves*
 1 *teaspoon salt*
 ½ *teaspoon freshly ground black pepper*

1. Pour the water into a saucepan, add the salt, and bring to a rolling boil. And the green beans. Cook at a rolling boil for 10 minutes, until the beans are tender yet still firm to the bite. Drain the green beans and transfer to a bowl. Cover the bowl and chill in the refrigerator.

2. When the beans are chilled, cut into 1-inch lengths. Return the beans to the bowl and add the olive oil, cider vinegar, minced garlic, and chopped cilantro.

3. Season to taste with salt and freshly ground black pepper.

4. Serve on chilled salad plates.

Notes and Variations

The salad is more attractive to the eye if placed on a lettuce leaf or topped with a cross of two pimento strips. Another vinegar can be used: tarragon, red wine, or balsamic. Another fresh herb can be used: basil, mint, or oregano.

. . . .

Lighter Version

Omit the olive oil and salt.
Add 1 more clove garlic.

	Regular		Lighter Version	
Calories:	158		39	
Protein:	2	g	2	g
Carbohydrates:	9	g	9	g
Dietary Fiber:	4	g	4	g
Fat:	13.5	g	<1	g
Cholesterol:	0	mg	0	mg
Sodium:	674	mg	7.5	mg

Percent of Calories

Protein:	5%		19%	
Carbohydrates:	21%		78%	
Fat:	73%		3%	

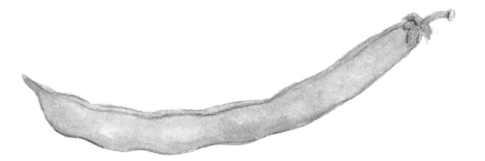

Hungarian Green Bean and Pea Salad

Serves 6

- 2 *quarts water*
- 1 *teaspoon salt*
- 1 *pound green beans, stringed and sliced in half lengthwise*
- 2 *cups fresh shelled peas*
- 1 *large carrot, diced*
- 1 *rib celery, diced*
- 5 *large raw egg yolks*
- 2 *tablespoons German mustard*
- 1½ *tablespoons sugar*
- 4 *tablespoons lemon juice*
- 1½ *cups sour cream*
- 1 *medium apple, diced*
- 1 *medium sour pickle, chopped*
- 1 *teaspoon salt*

1. In a saucepan, heat an inch of water with a teaspoon of salt until it boils. Add the green beans, fresh peas, and diced carrot and celery. Cover and cook at a simmer for 5 minutes, stirring occasionally. Don't overcook. Drain the vegetables and refrigerate.

2. In the top of a double boiler, combine the raw egg yolks with the German mustard, sugar, lemon juice, and sour cream. Cook over low heat, whisking constantly, until the sauce has thickened. Do not boil or the sauce will separate. Set aside.

3. Remove the cooled, cooked vegetables from the refrigerator and transfer to a bowl. Fold in the sauce and add the diced apple and chopped pickle.

4. Season to taste with salt.

. . . .

Notes and Variations

Hot dressing and cold vegetables? Yes — authentically Hungarian. This salad can be made using all green beans, 1½ pounds, if fresh peas are not available. Or good quality canned petits pois can be used instead of the fresh peas. Other mustards can replace the German mustard and a pear can replace the apple.

. . . .

Lighter Version

Omit the salt in the vegetable blanching water and in the seasoning. Eliminate the egg yolks and cooking of the dressing. Replace the 1½ cups regular sour cream with 2 cups nonfat sour cream. Simply combine all the dressing ingredients together before folding into the vegetables.

NUTRITIONAL ANALYSIS

	Regular		Lighter Version	
Calories:	272		182	
Protein:	8	g	9	g
Carbohydrates:	24	g	35	g
Dietary Fiber:	6	g	6	g
Fat:	16.5	g	<1	g
Cholesterol:	203	mg	0	mg
Sodium:	685	mg	263	mg

Percent of Calories

Protein:	12%	20%
Carbohydrates:	34%	79%
Fat:	54%	2%

ARMENIAN PICKLED
GREEN STRING BEANS

Serves 6 as hor d'oeuvres

1 *pound green string beans*

3 *tablespoons salt*

4 *cloves garlic, thinly sliced*

2 *hot red fresh or dried chiles*

1 *cup water*

¼ *cup distilled white vinegar*

1 *tablespoon sugar*

. . . .

1. Wash and string the beans. In a bowl, toss the string beans with
    2 tablespoons salt and allow to stand for 5 hours. Rinse the beans of the
    salt under running water and drain. Transfer the beans to a sterilized jar,
    adding the sliced garlic cloves and chiles.

2. In a stainless steel or enameled saucepan, combine the water and
    1 tablespoon salt. Heat and stir until the salt is completely dissolved.
    Add the white vinegar and the sugar and bring to a boil.

3. Remove from the heat and pour the pickling liquid into the bean jar
    and seal the jar tightly with a lid. Be sure the seal is airtight.

4. Keep the pickled green beans sealed in the jar for a week before using.
    Refrigerate after opening.

. . . .

Notes and Variations

Flavored vinegars like tarragon or raspberry make interesting alternative choices to distilled
white vinegar. This same recipe can be used for other fresh beans as well as dried beans that
have been cooked to a tender, not mushy stage.

. . . .

Lighter Version

Omit the salt altogether.
Omit the sugar.

NUTRITIONAL ANALYSIS

	Regular		Lighter Version	
Calories:	36		28	
Protein:	1.5	g	1.5	g
Carbohydrates:	9	g	6.7	g
Dietary Fiber:	2.5	g	2.5	g
Fat:	0	g	0	g
Cholesterol:	0	mg	0	mg
Sodium:	1072	mg	6.5	mg

Percent of Calories

Protein:	14 %	18 %
Carbohydrates:	83 %	79 %
Fat:	2 %	3 %

Hungarian Lamb and Green Bean Soup

Serves 6

2 slices bacon, diced

1 pound lean lamb, diced

1 small onion, minced

1½ quarts beef stock

¼ teaspoon caraway seeds

2 teaspoons Hungarian paprika

1 clove garlic, crushed

1 bay leaf

2 teaspoons salt

1 teaspoon freshly ground black pepper

2 tablespoons lard (traditional) or olive oil

2 tablespoons flour

1 pound fresh green beans, cut into 1-inch pieces

½ cup sour cream

1 tablespoon minced parsley

1. Heat a soup pot or large saucepan and add the diced bacon and render its fat.

2. Add the diced lamb and continue cooking until it is nicely browned.

3. Add the minced onion and cook until it just begins to color.

4. Add the beef stock and stir in the caraway seeds, Hungarian paprika, garlic, bay leaf, salt, and freshly ground black pepper. Cover and simmer gently for 30 minutes. Discard the bay leaf.

5. In a small saucepan, melt the lard and stir in the flour. Stir and cook this "roux" until it is lightly browned. Ladle out some of the cooking liquid from the soup pot and carefully whisk it into the roux. Stir the roux into the soup.

6. Add the green beans and simmer the soup until the beans are cooked, yet with a hint of crispness in the bite.

7. To serve, stir in the sour cream, adjust the seasonings if necessary, and stir in the minced parsley.

· ·

Notes and Variations

Water can be used here if there is no beef stock or broth. The ingredients are rich enough to produce a robust flavor. Another fat or oil can be used in place of the lard: butter, peanut oil, or olive oil. Any fresh pea or bean can be used in this recipe.

· ·

Lighter Version

Eliminate the bacon or substitute fat-free turkey bacon for the pork bacon. Omit the lard and salt. Substitute nonfat, low-sodium beef broth for the beef stock. Increase the caraway seeds by 1 teaspoon, the paprika by 2 teaspoons, the garlic by 2 cloves, add 2 more bay leaves, and increase the parsley by 2 tablespoons. Substitute nonfat sour cream for the regular sour cream. Instead of cooking the roux with lard and flour, simply cook the flour dry in a small pan, stirring constantly, until it is a light wood color. Then whisk in some of the soup liquid and add this into the soup itself.

NUTRITIONAL ANALYSIS

	Regular		Lighter Version	
Calories:	283		196	
Protein:	14.5	g	17	g
Carbohydrates:	10	g	14	g
Dietary Fiber:	3	g	3.5	g
Fat:	21	g	8.5	g
Cholesterol:	53.5	mg	37	mg
Sodium:	870	mg	118	mg

Percent of Calories

Protein:	20 %	34 %
Carbohydrates:	14 %	28 %
Fat:	66 %	38 %

TURKISH FRIED GREEN BEANS *Serves 4 as a side*

1 *pound fresh green beans*
6 *cups water*
2½ *teaspoons salt*
2 *tablespoons freshly squeezed lemon juice*
2 *eggs, beaten*
¼ *teaspoon freshly ground white pepper*
1 *cup dry bread crumbs*
Oil for deep frying
Hazelnut Sauce (page 344)

1. Rinse and string the green beans.

2. In a saucepan, combine the water, 2 teaspoons salt, and bring to a rolling boil. Add the lemon juice, return to a boil, and add the green beans. Bring to a boil again and boil for 2 minutes, until the beans are just beginning to become tender, yet remain crunchy to the bite. Drain the beans and place them on paper towels to dry.

3. In a bowl, beat the eggs together with ½ teaspoon salt and the white pepper. Add the blanched green beans and toss in the bowl until all are well coated with the seasoned eggs.

4. In another bowl, add the bread crumbs and toss in the egg-coated green beans until all the beans are coated with the bread crumbs.

5. In a frying pan or skillet, heat a 1-inch depth of oil to 375°F. Carefully add the beans to the heated oil without crowding the pan. Turn them as they cook to brown on all sides, about 2 minutes. Using a slotted spoon or spatula, transfer the cooked beans to a platter lined with absorbent paper to drain.

6. Serve hot with hazelnut sauce for dipping.

. . . .

Notes and Variations

Any fresh bean can be used in this recipe. The beans simply need to be cooked tender before the coatings begin. A good red wine vinegar can replace the lemon juice. Other sauces are good with this recipe; try garlic tahini or aïoli.

. . . .

Lighter Version

Omit the salt. Don't add the lemon juice to the blanching water. Sprinkle it over the beans after they come out of the oven. Increase the measure of lemon juice by 1 tablespoon. Replace the 2 raw eggs with 4 egg whites. In this recipe we will not fry the beans. Instead, after they are breaded, arrange on a nonstick baking sheet. Bake in a preheated 375°F oven for 10 minutes, until nicely browned.

NUTRITIONAL ANALYSIS

	Regular		Lighter Version	
Calories:	328		147	
Protein:	8	g	7.5	g
Carbohydrates:	27.5	g	27	g
Dietary Fiber:	5	g	5	g
Fat:	22	g	1.5	g
Cholesterol:	93.5	mg	0	mg
Sodium:	783	mg	255	mg

Percent of Calories

Protein:	10 %	19 %
Carbohydrates:	33 %	72 %
Fat:	58 %	9 %

. . . .

Other Green Bean Preparations

— Toss the cooked green beans with vinaigrette or flavored vinegar and serve hot or cold.

— Serve cold with olive oil, vinegar, strips of grilled bell peppers and chopped pecans, cashews, or pine nuts.

— Simmer undercooked beans in a tomato sauce with fresh chopped basil.

— Simmer cooked beans in a cream sauce.

— Simmer cooked beans in a salsa.

— Simmer with heavy cream and a dash of sherry.

— Simmer in chicken or beef bouillon.

— Puree cooked beans with one-quarter of its weight of cooked potatoes. Season with salt and pepper and add a little butter.

Flageolets

Shell Bean

Phaseolus vulgaris
ORIGIN: CENTRAL AMERICA

Flageolets or shell beans are simply any of the numerous common beans that have reached the stage of growth when the bean pod becomes tough, and the young bean within is sizable enough to be removed from the pod or shell and eaten fresh. These same beans will pass to the next stage and final stage of maturity as dried beans if they are left in the pod to complete their growth and then allowed to dry on the plant, in the field, or in the pod.

Shell beans can be taken from any of the common bean varieties, such as red bean, scarlet runner, black bean, and great Northern.

Since these beans are not dried, they do not need soaking. And since they are fresh, they can be cooked in a much shorter period of time than dried versions. A fresh shell bean can be cooked from as little as 12 minutes boiling time. The time varies according to the size and stage of maturity of the shell bean.

Not to confuse beans with "pea" varieties, the black-eyed pea, or crowder, is often available in the shell, fresh, or frozen state. The standard pea is also a "shelled" variety of pea.

Another area of shell beans is the immature bean taken from the pod fresh, then dried for packaging. In this way, a consumer can have the smaller immature bean when desired even when not fresh. This bean is most commonly referred to as a flageolet, or French flageolet. Most beans used as flageolets are immature white kidney beans removed from the pod.

In France the flageolet is most often served as an accompaniment to lamb.

Shell beans, flageolets, can be cooked as any green bean, pea, or dried bean, with less cooking time.

BOILED FLAGEOLETS, SHELL BEANS

Serves 4 as a side

Water to cover
4 *cups fresh beans*

. . . .

1. Bring the water to a boil.

2. Add the beans and boil for about 12 minutes, until tender.

. . . .

Notes and Variations

This simple recipe can be used for readying the beans to be used in any sauce or added combinations of seasoning vegetables or meats. I give the analysis without salt or other seasonings to show the pure bean content. These beans can also be steamed.

NUTRITIONAL ANALYSIS

Calories:	254	
Protein:	16	g
Carbohydrates:	46	g
Dietary Fiber:	14	g
Fat:	1	g
Cholesterol:	0	mg
Sodium:	3.5	mg

Percent of Calories

Protein:	25%
Carbohydrates:	71%
Fat:	4%

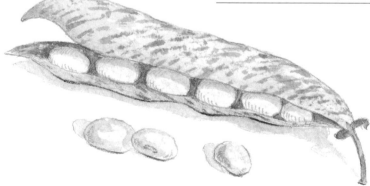

SAUTÉED FLAGEOLETS

Serves 4 as a side

4 *tablespoons butter*

4 *green onions, chopped*

1 *medium onion, chopped*

2 *cloves garlic, minced*

4 *cups fresh shelled young kidney beans*

1 *teaspoon salt*

½ *teaspoon white pepper*

. . . .

1. Heat the butter in a sauté pan and lightly sauté the green onions, onion, and garlic until soft.

2. Add the beans, cover and simmer for about 10 minutes, until the beans are cooked.

3. Season to taste with salt and white pepper.

. . . .

Notes and Variations

Bean cooking time will vary. Add a preferred herb, dry or fresh, to enhance the flavor. Tarragon is a good choice. If you cook the beans without the butter by adding only a little water or stock in its place, the fat will be reduced to less than 1 gram per serving, calories to 183, and cholesterol to 0.

NUTRITIONAL ANALYSIS

Calories:	252	
Protein:	11.5	g
Carbohydrates:	34	g
Dietary Fiber:	10	g
Fat:	8.5	g
Cholesterol:	21	mg
Sodium:	439	mg

Percent of Calories

Protein:	18%
Carbohydrates:	53%
Fat:	30%

FLAGEOLETS IN CORNMEAL WITH TOMATOES AND BACON

Serves 6 as an entree

1½ *quarts water, or enough to cover*
 1 *pound fresh flageolets, shell beans*
 6 *strips bacon, diced*
 1 *medium onion, thinly sliced*
 3 *cloves garlic, chopped*
 1 *large tomato, diced*
 1 *pound yellow cornmeal*
 1 *teaspoon salt*
 1 *teaspoon black pepper*

1. Bring the water to a boil and cook the shell beans for about 12 minutes, until tender. Drain the beans reserving the liquor and hold both aside.

2. In a pan, sauté the bacon until most of the fat is rendered.

3. Add the onion and garlic and sauté until lightly browned.

4. Add the tomato.

5. Add about 2½ cups of the bean water and bring to a boil.

6. Add the cornmeal, salt, and pepper, cover and simmer for about 20 minutes, until the cornmeal is cooked. Add more bean water if necessary during the cooking.

7. The resulting dish should spoon up fairly dry. If you need to dry the mixture more, uncover the pot and continue to simmer until all the liquid has dissipated.

Notes and Variations

Eliminate the bacon and calories are reduced to 401, the fat is reduced to less than 1 gram, and the cholesterol to 0. Add a fresh chopped herb to finish such as thyme, basil, or parsley.

NUTRITIONAL ANALYSIS

Calories:	653	
Protein:	12.5	g
Carbohydrates:	84	g
Dietary Fiber:	8.5	g
Fat:	29	g
Cholesterol:	29	mg
Sodium:	515	mg

Percent of Calories

Protein:	8%
Carbohydrates:	52%
Fat:	40%

Other Flageolet Preparations

— Serve cold as a salad tossed with chopped green onions and a vinaigrette.

— Combine with cooked green beans and serve as a salad or serve hot as a side dish.

— Puree as a soup base.

— Puree with one-quarter quantity of cooked potato as a side dish.

— Marinate in brine or seasoned pickles or marinate as appetizers or to be added to a salad.

— Sauté with bacon, ham, or prosciutto.

— Serve with tomato sauce or salsa.

— Boil with heavy cream.

Red Beans

Kidney Bean, Red Mexican Bean, Chili Bean, Red Haricot

Phaseolus vulgaris

ORIGIN: CENTRAL AMERICA

Red bean, black bean, white bean, pinto bean, green bean, snap bean, and string bean are all members of the same bean family. They are the best known to and most used by Americans and are used extensively throughout the world.

The red bean has probably found its most important place in the traditional New Orleans red beans and rice. It is used in Mexico and Central and South America as a chili bean, refried bean, and soup bean and in all European and Middle Eastern cuisines in soups and other hearty dishes.

BOILED RED BEANS

Serves 6 as a side

1 *pound red kidney beans, soaked*
8 *cups water*
4 *bay leaves*

· ·

Simmer the beans in the water with the bay leaves, covered, for
1½ hours, until they begin to tenderize. Discard the bay leaves. Serve.

· ·

Notes and Variations

I have not added salt so the analysis will
read only with the sodium in the beans.
If you add salt before the beans are tender,
it can cause the beans to take almost twice
as long to cook. Wait until they are beginning to tenderize, then season with salt.
Simply boiled like this, red beans can be
packed in a salt brine or vinaigrette-type
marinade for snacks. They can also be
added to salads, soups, and vegetable
dishes. Puree the beans with 1 cup boiled
potato and serve as puree. Cook them
tender before their skins begin to break,
and roast them quickly in the oven with a
little salt or soy for seasoning and eat
as you would peanuts.

NUTRITIONAL ANALYSIS

Calories:	228	
Protein:	15.5	g
Carbohydrates:	41	g
Dietary Fiber:	14	g
Fat:	<1	g
Cholesterol:	0	mg
Sodium:	2	mg

Percent of Calories

Protein:	27%
Carbohydrates:	70%
Fat:	3%

RED BEANS AND RICE

Serves 6 as an entree

1 pound red kidney beans, soaked
2 quarts water
2 tablespoons bacon drippings or corn oil
1 large onion, chopped
1 bunch green onions, chopped
1 bell pepper, seeded and chopped
4 cloves garlic, minced
1 pound smoked ham, cut into 1-inch cubes
3 bay leaves
1 teaspoon dried thyme leaves
2 tablespoons minced parsley
1 tablespoon vinegar
2 teaspoons salt
1 teaspoon freshly ground black pepper
6 cups hot cooked white rice

. . . .

1. Put the beans in a heavy soup pot with water. Bring the water to a boil and turn down to a simmer. Simmer for 1 hour.

2. In a sauté pan, heat the bacon drippings and sauté the onion, green onions, bell pepper, and garlic until they begin to color. Add to the bean pot.

3. In the same sauté pan, brown the smoked ham cubes. Add them and all the remaining seasoning ingredients to the bean pot.

4. Simmer for another ½ hour, until the beans are tender and have made their own thick sauce of the liquid in the pot. Add water to the pot if the beans become too dry before they are completely cooked.

5. Stir occasionally while cooking to prevent the beans from sticking to the bottom of the pot. Do this carefully with a wooden spoon so you don't break the beans.

   Adjust the seasonings, discard the bay leaves, and serve the beans spooned over hot cooked white rice.

Notes and Variations

Variations on this dish by the cooks of New Orleans are as many as there are cooks them-selves. Many different seasoning meats can be used: pickled pork, pork chops, sausage, salt pork, pigs' tails, bacon, tasso, and smoked meats. But ham is probably the most popular.

Lighter Version

Cook the seasoning vegetables dry in a pan, stirring constanatly, without the bacon. Replace the ham with low-fat turkey ham. Omit the salt. Double the measure of green onions and the garlic by 2 cloves. Cook the rice without adding salt, butter, or oil.

NUTRITIONAL ANALYSIS

	Regular		Lighter Version	
Calories:	723		410	
Protein:	39	g	22.5	g
Carbohydrates:	100	g	75	g
Dietary Fiber:	18.5	g	14	g
Fat:	18.5	g	2	g
Cholesterol:	74	mg	16	mg
Sodium:	2044	mg	299	mg

Percent of Calories

Protein:	20%	80%
Carbohydrates:	2%	15%
Fat:	78%	5%

RED BEANS
WITH BORDEAUX WINE

Serves 8 as a side

1   *pound dried red kidney beans, soaked*

6   *cups beef stock or water*

2   *cups red Bordeaux wine or other dry red wine*

2   *large onions, chopped*

2   *carrots, chopped*

2   *ribs celery, chopped*

1   *head garlic, chopped (10 to 12 cloves)*

2   *bay leaves*

1   *teaspoon dried thyme leaves*

2   *tablespoons minced parsley*

2   *teaspoons salt*

1   *teaspoon freshly ground black pepper*

1. Put the beans in a heavy soup pot with the beef stock or water and bring to a simmer. Simmer for 1½ hours, until tender. Add more stock or water but remember that red wine will also be added later.

2. Add the Bordeaux wine or other red wine along with the onions, carrots, celery, garlic, bay leaves, thyme, and parsley. Simmer for another hour, until the beans are very tender. Discard the bay leaves.

3. Season to taste with salt and black pepper.

. . . .

Notes and Variations

This is the traditional French red bean dish. If you don't have Bordeaux, use any other rich red wine of your choice. There is no reason why a white wine will not suffice. You may want to finish with some fresh chopped parsley and green onions. This most healthful recipe needs no fat reduction. Sodium in the beef broth or stock can be eliminated by using an unsalted stock.

NUTRITIONAL ANALYSIS

Calories:	245	
Protein:	13.5	g
Carbohydrates:	38	g
Dietary Fiber:	12	g
Fat:	1	g
Cholesterol:	0	mg
Sodium:	1422	mg

Percent of Calories

Protein:	21 %
Carbohydrates:	61 %
Fat:	3 %

RED BEAN AND TOMATO SOUP WITH PARMESAN CHEESE *Serves 8 as an entree soup*

1   *pound dried red haricot beans, presoaked and drained of soaking water*
12   *cups chicken stock or water*
4   *tablespoons butter*
2   *medium carrots, diced*
2   *medium onions, diced*
2   *medium turnips, diced*
6   *large tomatoes, diced*
4   *tablespoons tomato paste*
2   *bay leaves*
1   *large rib celery, minced*
2   *teaspoons salt*
1   *teaspoon white pepper*
2   *tablespoons chopped parsley*
2   *tablespoons fresh basil*
1   *cup grated Parmesan cheese*

1. Rinse the soaked red haricot beans and place in a soup pot with the chicken stock. Bring to a simmer, cover, and cook gently for 1½ hours, until the red beans begin to tenderize.

2. In a large sauté pan or skillet, melt the butter and sauté the diced carrots, onions, and turnips until they just begin to color. Add to the beans.

3. Add the diced tomatoes, tomato paste, bay leaves, and minced celery. Season with salt and white pepper.

4. Bring to a simmer, cover, and cook for another 45 minutes, until the beans are very tender.

5. Add the chopped parsley and basil.

6. Serve with 2 tablespoons of Parmesan sprinkled over the top of each soup bowl.

Notes and Variations

Using a salted chicken stock from the beginning of cooking may cause the beans to take longer to tenderize. Be patient. Use more chopped parsley and basil if you want a stronger herb taste. Other fresh herbs can also be used such as oregano and rosemary. Use only 1 tablespoon of these two herbs since they are stronger than parsley and basil. This soup can be pureed before serving for a smooth texture. Do so in batches in a blender and return to heat before serving.

Lighter Version

Omit the butter and salt. Replace the regular chicken stock with a nonfat, low-sodium chicken broth or water. Replace the Parmesan cheese with a nonfat Parmesan cheese. Increase the parsley and basil each by 2 tablespoons.

NUTRITIONAL ANALYSIS

	Regular	Lighter Version
Calories:	371	275
Protein:	21.5 g	19 g
Carbohydrates:	50 g	51 g
Dietary Fiber:	13.7 g	13.8 g
Fat:	11 g	1 g
Cholesterol:	25.5 mg	0 mg
Sodium:	2061 mg	150 mg

Percent of Calories

	Regular	Lighter Version
Protein:	22%	26%
Carbohydrates:	52%	70%
Fat:	26%	3%

RED BEAN, CRAB, AND LEEK SOUP   *Serves 8*

1   pound dried red haricot beans
12   cups water
4   raw crabs
4   tablespoons olive oil
3   large leeks, scrubbed and sliced
1   large onion, chopped
2   ribs celery, chopped
1   small green bell pepper, seeded and chopped
6   cloves garlic, chopped
4   bay leaves
1   teaspoon thyme leaves
2   teaspoons salt
1   teaspoon black pepper
½   teaspoon cayenne pepper
2   green onions, chopped
¼   cup chopped parsley

1. Soak and rinse the beans. Simmer in 12 cups of fresh water until tender.

2. Remove the top shells of the crabs and quarter them. Remove and discard the gray feathery lungs. Crack the legs and claws lightly with a knife so all the juices will be released into the beans during cooking. Add to the beans, including any liquid and fat resulting from the process.

3. In a sauté pan, heat the olive oil and sauté the chopped leeks, onion, celery, bell pepper, garlic, and bay leaves until the vegetables brown slightly. Add to the bean pot.

4. Add the thyme, salt, black pepper, and cayenne. Simmer for 20 minutes. Discard the bay leaves.

5. Remove and discard the crab top shells. Adjust the seasonings if desired and add the chopped green onions and parsley and serve in soup bowls with 2 quarter crabs in each bowl.

· ·

Notes and Variations

Any haricot beans can be used here: red, white, or black. I use all of the leek, green and white. The green will remain more firm, while the white softens. It gives the final dish a nice variation in texture. Soft-shell crabs can be used as well as hard. Be sure to lift up the soft top shell to remove and discard the lungs before cooking. Louisiana dry or liquid seafood boil seasoning can be used to your taste to give this dish a more familiar seafood flavor.

· ·

Lighter Version

Omit the olive oil and salt. Increase the measure of garlic by 3 cloves, the bay leaves by 2, and the thyme by 1 teaspoon. Add 1 tablespoon fresh lemon juice to finish.

NUTRITIONAL ANALYSIS

	Regular		Lighter Version	
Calories:	305		248	
Protein:	18	g	18	g
Carbohydrates:	42	g	43	g
Dietary Fiber:	13	g	13	g
Fat:	8	g	1.5	g
Cholesterol:	24	mg	24	mg
Sodium:	633	mg	101	mg

Percent of Calories

Protein:	23%	28%
Carbohydrates:	54%	67%
Fat:	23%	5%

RED BEANS WITH TURNIPS AND GREENS AND PICKLED PORK

Serves 6.

1 *pound red haricot beans, soaked and rinsed*

1½ *quarts water*

1 *pound pickled pork shoulder, cut into 6 slices*

4 *bay leaves*

1 *teaspoon freshly ground black pepper*

¼ *teaspoon cayenne pepper*

1 *bunch turnips and greens, scrubbed and rinsed*

1 *large yellow onion, chopped*

4 *cloves garlic*

2 *teaspoons salt*

. . . .

1. Combine the red beans and water in a bean pot. Add the pickled pork, bay leaves, black pepper, and cayenne. Bring slowly to a simmer, skim off and discard the foam, cover, and cook for 1 hour, until the beans just begin to tenderize.

2. Cut the turnip greens into 1½-inch lengths and dice the turnips. Use all of the turnips and greens, even the tough lower leaf stems.

3. Add the turnips and greens, yellow onion, garlic and salt to taste. Cover and simmer for another ½ hour, until the vegetables are cooked but not overly so, and the beans are very tender to the bite. Discard the bay leaves.

4. Taste for salt and pepper, adjust if desired, and serve.

. . . .

Notes and Variations

The pickled pork can also be cubed or left in a single piece during the cooking, then sliced to serve. Ham can replace the pickled pork, as well as fresh pork roast. Add water as needed, but not too much before the vegetables are added: They release and add their own water. This recipe can be served over any kind of rice, barley, or other grains.

. . . .

Lighter Version

For an even more healthful version of this recipe, omit the pickled pork and salt. Replace the water with nonfat, low-sodium chicken or beef bouillon. Fill out the flavors of this recipe by adding the following: 2 bay leaves, 1 teaspoon dried thyme leaves, 1 yellow onion, 4 cloves garlic, and 1 tablespoon red wine vinegar.

NUTRITIONAL ANALYSIS

	Regular		Lighter Version	
Calories:	403		334	
Protein:	35	g	23	g
Carbohydrates:	53	g	57	g
Dietary Fiber:	17	g	17	g
Fat:	6	g	2.5	g
Cholesterol:	53	mg	0	mg
Sodium:	978	mg	120	mg

Percent of Calories

Protein:	34%	27%
Carbohydrates:	52%	66%
Fat:	14%	7%

PORTUGUESE PEASANT SOUP

Serves 12

1 *pound dried red kidney beans, soaked*

3 *quarts chicken stock or more, if necessary*

12 *strips thick-sliced smoked bacon, diced*

1 *pound chorizo or other smoked pork sausage, sliced*

3 *medium yellow onions, chopped*

6 *cloves garlic, minced*

3 *medium potatoes, scrubbed and diced*

4 *medium carrots, scrubbed and diced*

4 *medium turnips, scrubbed and diced*

1 *small cabbage, cored and chopped*

4 *bay leaves*

1 *tablespoon salt*

2 *teaspoons freshly ground black pepper*

1 *cup chopped cilantro*

1. Simmer the beans in the chicken stock for about 2 hours, or until they begin to tenderize.

2. In a saucepan or soup pot, sauté the diced bacon until it has rendered its fat. Add the chorizo, onions, garlic and sauté until they begin to color.

3. Add the diced potatoes, carrots, turnips, cabbage, bay leaves, and cilantro. Season with salt and pepper. Bring to a simmer and cook for another ½ hour, until the vegetables are tender. Add the cilantro before serving.

. . . .

Notes and Variations

Add more stock or water during cooking if the soup becomes too thick. This is a hearty rustic soup reminiscent of Portuguese countryside cooking. It can be made without the meats and stock for a substantial vegetarian version.

. . . .

Lighter Version

Omit the bacon, chorizo, and salt. Replace the chicken stock with a low-fat stock or water. Add the raw vegetables directly to the beans after they tenderize.

NUTRITIONAL ANALYSIS

	Regular		Lighter Version	
Calories:	534		239	
Protein:	29	g	17	g
Carbohydrates:	43	g	42	g
Dietary Fiber:	11.5	g	11.5	g
Fat:	29	g	<1	g
Cholesterol:	53	mg	0	mg
Sodium:	2135	mg	225	mg

Percent of Calories

Protein:	21%		28%	
Carbohydrates:	31%		69%	
Fat:	48%		3%	

INDIAN RED BEAN RAJMA

Serves 6

  1 *pound dried red beans, soaked*
  8 *cups water*
  ¼ *cup olive oil*
  1 *large onion, chopped*
  4 *cloves garlic, chopped*
  1 *tablespoon minced fresh ginger*
  3 *large tomatoes, diced*
  1 *teaspoon ground turmeric*
  2 *teaspoons salt*
  1 *teaspoon Garam Masala (see recipe)*
  ½ *cup chopped fresh cilantro*

1. Simmer the soaked red beans in the water until tender, 1 to 1½ hours.

2. In a sauté pan, heat the olive oil and sauté the onion, garlic, and ginger until they begin to color.

3. Add the diced tomatoes to the onion mixture and simmer for 5 minutes more. Add to the red beans.

4. Season with turmeric, salt, and Garam Masala, and continue simmering until the beans are very tender and the liquid is somewhat reduced and thickened.

5. Fold in the chopped fresh cilantro and serve.

Notes and Variations

As with many of the recipes in this book, this one can be made quite successfully with almost any other pulse — try this with lentils or chickpeas. The recipe can also be served over a starch — rice or couscous — and will serve more people.

Lighter Version

Omit the olive oil and salt. Increase the Garam Masala by ½ teaspoon. Add 2 tablespoons fresh lemon juice just before serving.

NUTRITIONAL ANALYSIS

	Regular		Lighter Version	
Calories:	368		290	
Protein:	18	g	18	g
Carbohydrates:	54	g	54	g
Dietary Fiber:	16	g	16	g
Fat:	10	g	1	g
Cholesterol:	0	mg	0	mg
Sodium:	729	mg	19	mg

Percent of Calories

Protein:	19 %		24 %	
Carbohydrates:	57 %		72 %	
Fat:	24 %		4 %	

Garam Masala, a Middle Eastern seasoning mix *Makes 2 ½ teaspoons*

Garam Masala is traditionally made from whole spice seeds and cinnamon bark, pan roasted briefly, and then ground into a powder. In this recipe I am simply adding the spice combination in mixed ground form. The resulting flavor in the dish is nearly imperceptible from the more complicated original.

- 1 teaspoon ground cinnamon
- ¼ teaspoon ground cardamom seeds
- ⅛ teaspoon ground cloves
- 1 teaspoon ground cumin
- ⅛ teaspoon ground nutmeg

Combine the ingredients and store in a small, tightly capped container. Use for seasoning Middle Eastern recipes or other recipes of your choice.

VENETIAN RED BEAN AND ANGEL HAIR PASTA SOUP

Serves 10

- 1 pound dried red beans, soaked
- 12 cups water
- 2 large onions, chopped
- 4 cloves garlic, minced
- ½ pound salt pork, chopped
- 4 tablespoons green and fruity olive oil
- ¼ teaspoon cinnamon
- 1 pound angel hair pasta, broken into 2-inch lengths
- 2 teaspoons salt or to taste
- 1½ teaspoons freshly ground black pepper
- 1 cup grated Parmesan cheese

1. Combine the soaked red beans and water in a soup pot and bring to a simmer.

2. Add the chopped onions, garlic, salt pork, olive oil, and cinnamon. Simmer for 1 to 1½ hours, until the beans are tender.

3. Add the pasta and season with salt and pepper. Simmer for 8 minutes, until the pasta is cooked.

4. To serve, ladle the soup into bowls and sprinkle with Parmesan cheese.

Notes and Variations

Notice that in this recipe the olive oil is used for flavor and texture and not as a cooking medium. Use an olive oil that has a fresh fruity flavor. Prosciutto makes an elegant exchange for the salt pork. Another pasta of your preference can be used in place of the angel hair. A richer soup can be made with a chicken or beef stock in place of the water. If the stock is salted, the beans will take longer to tenderize. Add more liquid when cooking the pasta if necessary.

Lighter Version

Omit the salt pork, olive oil, and salt. Use low-fat Parmesan cheese in place of the regular. Add ½ cup minced green olives.

NUTRITIONAL ANALYSIS

	Regular		Lighter Version	
Calories:	473		345	
Protein:	22	g	19	g
Carbohydrates:	61	g	64	g
Dietary Fiber:	10.5	g	10.5	g
Fat:	16	g	2	g
Cholesterol:	16.7	mg	8	mg
Sodium:	739	mg	138	mg

Percent of Calories

Protein:	19%	22%
Carbohydrates:	51%	73%
Fat:	30%	5%

. . . .

Other Red Bean Preparations

— Prepare red beans as a salad, adding chopped onion, fresh lettuce, and tomatoes.
  Serve with your preferred salad dressing.

— Three bean salad can be prepared with your choice of cooked and chilled beans.
  Use red and white and string beans; red and black limas; favas, cannellini,
  and red beans, with your choice of dressing.

— Sauté the cooked drained beans with butter and garnish with fresh herbs.

— Bake the cooked, drained beans in a gratin dish with a little heavy cream, and top
  with bread crumbs and Parmesan, Gruyère, or Swiss cheese.

— Puree cooked red beans and heat to thicken enough to hold its shape.
  Add a little cream or butter for richness.

— Simmer in your favorite tomato sauce.

— Add to stir-fry dishes and tofu recipes.

— Add cooked red beans to any soup.

Black Beans

Turtle Bean

Phaseolus vulgaris
ORIGIN: CENTRAL AMERICA

Black bean or turtle bean is a member of the same family as the red bean, white bean, and green bean. It has become very popular in the United States due to the infusion of Cuban, Mexican, Central and South American, Brazilian and Caribbean cuisines into our own cuisine.

The black bean can be used in any recipe that calls for red or white bean; the recipe's resulting flavor is preferred by many.

The black bean is being studied for its peculiar properties, which claim to aid in the prevention of breast and prostate cancer. It is also said to reduce the craving for alcohol.

BOILED BLACK BEANS

Serves 6 as a side or an entree

1 *pound black beans, soaked*
8 *cups water*
4 *bay leaves*
   Salt, to taste
   Freshly ground black pepper, to taste

. . . .

1. Cook the beans in the water with the bay leaves at a simmer for 45 minutes, until tender.

2. Season to taste and serve.

. . . .

Notes and Variations

The smaller the beans, the faster they will cook. This serving is substantial, about 1 full cup of beans per serving. The analysis is given without salt added so you can see the natural sodium in black beans.

NUTRITIONAL ANALYSIS

Calories:	237	
Protein:	16	g
Carbohydrates:	43	g
Dietary Fiber:	15.5	g
Fat:	1	g
Cholesterol:	0	mg
Sodium:	11	mg

Percent of Calories

Protein:	26 %
Carbohydrates:	70 %
Fat:	4 %

CURRIED BLACK BEAN AND ORANGE SALAD

Serves 6

6   *cups cooked black beans, chilled (or cook 1 pound dried beans)*

4   *large oranges, sectioned and seeded*

2   *medium red onions, thinly sliced*

2   *limes, juice only*

½   *cup cider vinegar*

1   *tablespoon curry powder*

¼   *cup chopped fresh cilantro*

2   *teaspoons salt*

2   *teaspoons habanero hot pepper sauce*

1. Combine the beans, oranges, and onions in a salad bowl.

2. Add all the remaining ingredients, tossing gently but thoroughly without breaking up the beans.

3. Adjust seasonings if desired and serve.

Notes and Variations

This salad can be made with any bean once it is cooked. The orange can be replaced with grapefruit or mandarin, or another sweet citrus fruit. All seasoning ingredients can be adjusted to suit your personal palate. There is no oil in this recipe, but feel free to add it if you desire.

NUTRITIONAL ANALYSIS

Calories:	317	
Protein:	18	g
Carbohydrates:	63	g
Dietary Fiber:	19	g
Fat:	1.5	g
Cholesterol:	0	mg
Sodium:	715	mg

Percent of Calories

Protein:	21%
Carbohydrates:	75%
Fat:	4%

BLACK BEANS AND RICE

Serves 6 as an entree

  1 *pound black beans, soaked*
  8 *cups water*
  ¼ *cup olive oil*
  2 *large onions, chopped*
  4 *cloves garlic, chopped*
  1 *large bell pepper, chopped*
  3 *large tomatoes, chopped*
  2 *cups uncooked short-grain rice*
  2 *teaspoons salt*
  1 *teaspoon black pepper*
  ¼ *teaspoon cayenne pepper*
  ¼ *cup chopped parsley*
  3 *green onions, chopped*

1. In a bean pot, simmer the beans in the water until cooked but not overly tender. Turn off the heat.

2. In a sauté pan, heat the olive oil and sauté the onions, garlic, and bell pepper. Simmer until they just begin to brown. Add the tomatoes and simmer together for 2 minutes. Add to the bean pot.

3. Add 2 cups fresh water to the bean pot and bring to a simmer. Add the uncooked rice to the bean pot and season the beans with salt, black pepper, and cayenne. Bring back to a simmer and cook for 20 minutes, until the rice is done. If you need more water to cook the rice, add it. If there is too much liquid when the rice is tender, uncover the pot and let the remaining liquid reduce.

4. Serve the black beans and rice garnished with parsley and green onions.

Notes and Variations

The Cubans and Spanish call this dish Moros y Cristianos. The Moors and Christians represent the Moorish invasion of Spain, black into white. This is a fairly simple rendition open to any additional garnish or increase of seasonings if desired. Serve with a good habanero hot pepper sauce. Omitting the olive oil reduces the fat to less than 2 grams per serving and the calorie count to 468.

NUTRITIONAL ANALYSIS

Calories:	530	
Protein:	21	g
Carbohydrates:	90	g
Dietary Fiber:	18	g
Fat:	10.5	g
Cholesterol:	0	mg
Sodium:	730	mg

Percent of Calories

Protein:	15 %
Carbohydrates:	67 %
Fat:	18 %

BLACK BEAN PUREE WITH COCONUT MILK

Serves 8 as a side or an appetizer

1 *pound black beans, soaked overnight*

6 *cups water*

1 *cup coconut milk*

2 *teaspoons salt*

½ *teaspoon freshly ground black pepper*

¼ *teaspoon cayenne pepper*

1. Simmer the beans in the water until very soft, 1½ to 2 hours. Add more water during the cooking, if necessary. Drain the cooked beans, reserving the cooking liquor.

2. In a blender or food processor container, combine the soft-cooked black beans with the coconut milk and puree. Add small amounts of the cooking liquor as needed to process the beans into a smooth puree.

3. Transfer the puree to a saucepan and simmer for a few minutes to reduce the liquid and thicken the puree. Stir regularly with a wooden spoon, being careful so that it does not stick to the bottom of the pan during this reduction process.

4. Season to taste with salt, freshly ground black pepper, and cayenne.

5. When the bean puree has thickened sufficiently, spoon it into small bowls to serve.

· ·

Notes and Variations

The coconut milk can be canned or fresh. You can also use ½ cup grated coconut, preferably fresh, in place of the coconut milk. The coconut milk gives the bean puree a very "buttery" flavor. Ground habanero pepper can be used in this recipe in place of the cayenne. It is not always easy to find, even in specialty shops. A squeeze of lime is nice here, as is a sprinkling of chopped cilantro and green onion.

· ·

Lighter Version

Omit the coconut milk and salt. Replace the coconut milk with 1 teaspoon of grated fresh coconut and a pinch of freshly ground nutmeg as a garnish on each serving of bean puree.

NUTRITIONAL ANALYSIS

	Regular		Lighter Version	
Calories:	234		187	
Protein:	12.5	g	12	g
Carbohydrates:	33	g	32.5	g
Dietary Fiber:	12	g	12	g
Fat:	9	g	1.5	g
Cholesterol:	0	mg	0	mg
Sodium:	547	mg	11	mg

Percent of Calories

Protein:	21%		25%	
Carbohydrates:	54%		68%	
Fat:	25%		7%	

BLACK BEAN SOUP

Serves 8

1   *pound dried black beans, soaked*
10 *cups water*
 2 *bay leaves*
¼ *cup fragrant olive oil*
 2 *cloves garlic, minced*
 2 *teaspoons salt*
½ *teaspoon freshly ground black pepper*

1. Simmer the beans in the water with the bay leaves, covered, for 1 hour, until very soft.

2. Heat the olive oil in a small saucepan and brown the garlic. Add the garlic and oil to the beans and simmer briefly.

3. Remove and discard the bay leaves and carefully transfer the garlic-flavored beans to a blender or food processor container, in batches if necessary, and process into a liquid.

4. Transfer the soup back into the soup pot. Add additional water, if desired, for a thin consistency. Bring to a simmer.

5. Season to taste with salt and freshly ground black pepper.

Notes and Variations

You can use any dried haricot bean or pea in this recipe. This is the simplest of recipes and can be enhanced by any additions you may choose. Try folding a tablespoon or so of a chopped fresh herb at the end, say, parsley, cilantro, or basil, or a squeeze of lime or lemon.

Lighter Version

Omit the olive oil and salt. Use 4 cloves minced garlic, 4 bay leaves, and 1 teaspoon dried thyme leaves and add directly to the beans after the beans have simmered for 30 minutes. Remember to remove the bay leaves before the soup is pureed.

NUTRITIONAL ANALYSIS

	Regular		Lighter Version	
Calories:	239		182	
Protein:	12	g	12	g
Carbohydrates:	32	g	33	g
Dietary Fiber:	12	g	12	g
Fat:	7.5	g	<1	g
Cholesterol:	0	mg	0	mg
Sodium:	543	mg	10	mg

Percent of Calories

Protein:	20%	26%
Carbohydrates:	53%	70%
Fat:	28%	4%

BLACK BEAN SOUP WITH HAM AND SHERRY

Serves 8

1 *pound black beans, soaked*
10 *cups water*
8 *ounces smoked ham, diced*
2 *medium onions, chopped*
2 *ribs celery, chopped*
½ *teaspoon ground cloves*
2 *teaspoons salt or to taste*
1 *teaspoon freshly ground black pepper*
¼ *teaspoon cayenne pepper*
¼ *cup dry sherry*
2 *tablespoons freshly squeezed lemon juice*
2 *hard-boiled eggs, chopped*

1. Combine the soaked black beans with the water and simmer, covered, for 1 hour.

2. Add the diced smoked ham to the beans along with the chopped onions, celery, and cloves. Season with the salt, black pepper, and cayenne. Continue simmering for another hour, until the black beans are very soft.

3. Carefully transfer the hot beans to a blender or food processor container and process into a liquid. Do this in batches if necessary. Return the "soup" to the saucepan and bring to a simmer.

4. Adjust the seasonings, if desired, and add the dry sherry and lemon juice. More water can be added if a thinner soup consistency is desired.

   To serve the soup, ladle into bowls and top each serving with a sprinkle of chopped hard-boiled eggs.

. . . .

Notes and Variations

The water added will vary according to the thickness desired of the soup. Other seasoning meats such as pickled pork, bacon, or smoked sausage can be used in place of the ham. The sherry and egg are not absolutely necessary, but add greatly to the finished soup. Another nice garnish to top the soup is a thin slice of lemon.

. . . .

Lighter Version

Omit the ham and salt. Replace the garnish of 2 chopped hard-boiled eggs with 4 hard-boiled egg whites. Add 2 cloves chopped garlic and 4 bay leaves when the vegetables are added to the beans. Remove the bay leaves.

NUTRITIONAL ANALYSIS

	Regular		Lighter Version	
Calories:	259		207	
Protein:	20	g	14	g
Carbohydrates:	36	g	36	g
Dietary Fiber:	12	g	13	g
Fat:	4	g	<1	g
Cholesterol:	68	mg	0	mg
Sodium:	999	mg	44	mg

Percent of Calories

Protein:	31%		26%
Carbohydrates:	54%		68%
Fat:	13%		4%

AFRICAN BLACK BEAN GUMBO *Serves 6 as an entree*

- 1 pound black beans, soaked overnight
- 8 cups water or unsalted beef stock
- 3 cups coconut milk
- 2 teaspoons salt
- 1 teaspoon cayenne pepper
- 1 dozen strips bacon, diced
- 6 Spanish chorizo sausages, halved lengthwise
- 3 cups sliced fresh okra
- 2 large onions, chopped
- 4 ribs celery, chopped
- ⅓ cup chopped fresh cilantro
- 12 cloves garlic, chopped
- 2 tablespoons red palm kernel oil
- ½ cup African ground shrimp (sometimes called crayfish)
- 2 cups short grain rice
- 4 cups water
- 1 tablespoon red palm kernel oil
- 2 teaspoons salt or less to taste

1. In a bean pot, simmer the soaked beans in the water or unsalted beef stock for 1 hour, until tender yet still retaining a bite to the texture. Drain and retain the liquid. Add the coconut milk to the beans and season with salt and cayenne.

2. In a sauté pan or skillet, sauté the diced bacon and chorizo sausages until all the fat is rendered from the bacon. Transfer the sausages to the bean pot.

3. Add the sliced okra, chopped onions, celery, and cilantro to the sauté pan with the bacon and fat and sauté until browned. Transfer to the bean pot.

4. Add the garlic and red palm kernel oil to the beans. Cook for another ½ hour, stirring occasionally and adding more water or beef stock as necessary, until the beans are tender and the sauce is thick.

5. Make the rice in a saucepan by combining it with the water, red palm kernel oil, and salt to taste. Bring to a simmer, cover, and cook for 20 minutes, until the rice is tender and the water absorbed.

6. Before serving the black bean gumbo, check for cayenne hotness and season with salt. There is salt in the bacon, sausages, and the ground shrimp so do not oversalt.

7. Serve over rice in large soup bowls.

. . . .

Notes and Variations

Canned or frozen okra can be used if the fresh is unavailable. The chorizo can be replaced with another sausage and the African ground shrimp can be replaced with dried shrimp. Dried shrimp has a much stronger flavor than fresh, and that strong flavor is a desired part of this dish. Chicken or shellfish stock can be used in place of beef stock. The red palm kernel oil is not absolutely necessary. It is, however, an ingredient that helps make this dish distinctive. Medium or long-grain white rice or brown rice can be used.

. . . .

Lighter Version

The liberal use of bacon combined with the oil and chorizo make this recipe absolutely delicious, but perhaps a bit fat heavy for many. Omit the fats and fat-laden products. Omit the bacon, chorizo, red palm kernel oil, and salt. Since the coconut milk gives the dish its distinctive buttery flavor, omit only 2 cups. Add an onion, ¼ cup chopped cilantro, and ½ cup dried shrimp.

NUTRITIONAL ANALYSIS

	Regular		Lighter Version	
Calories:	933		422	
Protein:	38	g	19.5	g
Carbohydrates:	72	g	71	g
Dietary Fiber:	15	g	15	g
Fat:	58	g	7.5	g
Cholesterol:	74	mg	20.8	mg
Sodium:	1599	mg	56	mg

Percent of Calories

Protein:	16%	18%
Carbohydrates:	31%	66%
Fat:	53%	16%

BRAZILIAN BLACK BEAN AND PORK STEW

Serves 8

  1 *pound dried black beans, soaked overnight*
  8 *cups water*
  8 *chorizo sausages*
  1 *pound pork shoulder*
  8 *ounces lean smoked slab bacon*
  8 *ounces pickled pork*
⅓ *cup olive oil*
  1 *minced habanero pepper or to taste*
  2 *limes, juiced*
  2 *large onions, chopped*
  8 *cloves garlic, chopped*
  2 *ribs celery, chopped*
  4 *bay leaves*
½ *cup chopped parsley*
  1 *teaspoon dried thyme*
  2 *teaspoons salt or to taste*
  1 *teaspoon freshly ground black pepper*
  8 *cups hot cooked fluffy white rice*

1. In a soup pot, combine the soaked beans, water, chorizo sausages, pork shoulder, smoked bacon, pickled pork, olive oil, habanero pepper, lime juice, chopped onions, chopped garlic, chopped celery, bay leaves, parsley, and thyme. Bring slowly to a simmer, cover, and cook for 1 hour, until the meats are very tender. The meats will cook tender at varying times, so check them as the beans simmer, removing each as it becomes tender. Slice the meats into 8 pieces each, except for the chorizo sausages which should be left whole.

2. Season the beans with salt and freshly ground black pepper. Continue simmering the beans for another hour, until they are tender.

3. Return the sliced meats and chorizo sausages to the bean pot, cover

and simmer for 10 minutes more, or long enough for all the meats to reheat. Remove the bay leaves.

4. Serve the beans over hot fluffy white rice in individual bowls with a slice of each meat and a sausage laid over the top.

. . . .

Notes and Variations

This is a version of the Brazilian national dish, the feijoada. It is even more important to Brazil than red beans and rice is to New Orleans and cassoulet to France. Use pork butt or shoulder if it is available. Use smoked pork roast if it is available. All this meat is not absolutely necessary. Use fewer kinds if you wish. Chorizo is a Spanish-style sausage. You can find it more easily packed in tins in food specialty shops or sold freshly made in sausage shops. Use sliced bacon if no slab bacon is available. The habanero pepper is a Caribbean pepper, also called Scotch bonnet pepper, the hottest pepper in the world. Use just the flesh and discard the seeds. The habanero pepper can be fresh or dried. Or use a hot sauce made with the same pepper. And wash your hands after handling the pepper!

. . . .

Lighter Version

Omit the chorizo sausages and bacon, along with the olive oil and salt. Try to find smoked pork shoulder or butt, and make sure it is lean and trimmed of all fat. Add a dash of liquid smoke flavor if you have it. The resulting dish is quite good with no other additions.

NUTRITIONAL ANALYSIS

	Regular		Lighter Version	
Calories:	1044		599	
Protein:	53	g	37	g
Carbohydrates:	96	g	95	g
Dietary Fiber:	14	g	14	g
Fat:	48.4	g	7	g
Cholesterol:	114	mg	49	mg
Sodium:	1827	mg	474	mg

	Percent of Calories			
Protein:	20%		25%	
Carbohydrates:	37%		64%	
Fat:	42%		11%	

BLACK TURTLE BEANS AND RICE

Serves 6 as an entree

Spice bag ingredients
6   whole cloves
6   whole allspice
1   teaspoon whole mustard seeds
1   teaspoon red pepper flakes

---

1   pound black turtle beans, soaked
2   quarts water
2   large white or yellow onions, chopped
1   bell pepper, seeded and chopped
1   bunch green onions, chopped
3   stalks celery, chopped
1   head garlic, minced (approximately 12 cloves)
4   bay leaves
1   teaspoon thyme
1   teaspoon grated lemon zest
2   tablespoons minced parsley
2   teaspoons salt or to taste
1   teaspoon freshly ground black pepper or to taste
¼   cup sherry
2   tablespoons lemon juice
6   cups hot cooked white rice

1. Make a spice bag by tying the ingredients into a piece of cheesecloth. This aids in the retrieval of the spices after cooking.

2. Put the beans in a heavy soup pot with the water, spice bag, and all the remaining ingredients except the sherry, lemon juice, and rice. Bring the water to a boil, turn down to a simmer, and cook for 1½ hours, stirring occasionally, until the beans are tender and have

made their own thick gravy from the pot liquor. Add water to the pot if the beans become too dry before they are completely cooked.

3. Adjust the seasonings if desired.

4. Add the sherry and lemon juice to the beans. Let simmer for a minute more.

5. Serve the beans spooned out over hot fluffy cooked white rice.

. . . .

Notes and Variations

This recipe is one that my great, great-grandfather Antoine Alciatore, founder of Antoine's restaurant in New Orleans, served as his special home-style black bean dish on fast days when no meat was consumed. It is no coincidence that he used a recipe similar for preparing actual turtle for the unrelated turtle beans. Since there is no meat in this recipe it is a marvelous dish for a fancy no-meat meal. There is also no added fat so the dish is low fat with no cholesterol. You may prefer, as I do, a brown rice for better nutrition. Try it with wild rice for a haute bean dish.

NUTRITIONAL ANALYSIS

Calories:	568	
Protein:	23	g
Carbohydrates:	112	g
Dietary Fiber:	19	g
Fat:	1.7	g
Cholesterol:	0	mg
Sodium:	737	mg

Percent of Calories

Protein:	16%
Carbohydrates:	79%
Fat:	3%

BOURBON
BLACK BEAN PIE

Yield: One 9-inch pie Serves 8

3   *eggs*
1   *cup sugar*
⅔   *cup dark corn syrup*
2   *tablespoons melted butter*
1   *teaspoon vanilla extract*
¼   *teaspoon salt*
¼   *cup bourbon*
2   *cups cooked unsalted black beans*
1   *frozen 9-inch piecrust*

1. In a bowl, beat the eggs together with the sugar, corn syrup, melted butter, vanilla, salt, and bourbon.

2. Fold in the black beans.

3. Pour the mixture into the piecrust, and bake the pie in a preheated 400°F oven for 10 minutes. Lower the heat to 350° and cook for about another 30 minutes, until the filling is set and the crust is browned.

4. Cool the pie on a wire rack and serve at room temperature.

Notes and Variations

This is a traditional recipe for pecan pie. You'll be surprised how delicious this pie is with black beans. Serve it with vanilla ice cream or whipped cream. Try this recipe with any dried bean. It works well without bourbon. Add a teaspoon dried ginger instead.

To create a lighter version of this recipe would simply undo this dish. Enjoy this as is for the delightful use of black beans.

NUTRITIONAL ANALYSIS

Calories:	376	
Protein:	7.5	g
Carbohydrates:	65	g
Dietary Fiber:	4	g
Fat:	10	g
Cholesterol:	105	mg
Sodium:	227	mg

Percent of Calories

Protein:	8%
Carbohydrates:	67%
Fat:	24%

Other Black Bean Preparations

— As salad with white and red beans and a good homemade vinaigrette or a favorite bottled dressing.

— As cold salad with jícama, onion, and cilantro.

— Pureed with potatoes.

— As garnish to soups and hearty bowl dishes.

— Baked with heavy cream and Mexican cheeses.

— Use in refried bean recipes.

— Serve as a side dish instead of rice.

— Keep a container of boiled, cooked beans at the ready in the refrigerator to add to any dish whenever you want — without the long cooking process. This will reawaken your ideas to the many uses of beans, especially those you have not thought of.

White Beans

*Great Northern, White Kidney,
Cannellini, Navy Pea*

Phaseolus vulgaris
ORIGIN: CENTRAL AMERICA

White beans are members of the same family of beans as the red bean, black bean, green bean, and so on. They are as widely popular in the United States as the red or black kidney bean, perhaps even more so, and is the most used kidney bean in Europe, Spain, and Italy. The white bean is more universally used than the red and black bean.

BOILED WHITE BEANS

Serves 6

1   *pound white beans, soaked*
8   *cups water*
    Salt, to taste
    Freshly ground black pepper, to taste

. . . .

1. Simmer the beans in the water until tender, about 1½ hours.

2. Season to taste with salt and pepper.

3. Use as is or add additional ingredients.

. . . .

Notes and Variations

White beans come in many sizes.
Cooking times can vary considerably.
The analysis is given here without salt
or fat added so you can see the bean's
nutritional elements.

NUTRITIONAL ANALYSIS

Calories:	250	
Protein:	17.5	g
Carbohydrates:	45	g
Dietary Fiber:	11.5	g
Fat:	<1	g
Cholesterol:	0	mg
Sodium:	11	mg

Percent of Calories

Protein:	27%
Carbohydrates:	70%
Fat:	2%

WHITE BEANS AND RICE   *Serves 6 as a hearty entree*

1 pound white beans, soaked

10 cups water

2 strips bacon, chopped, or 2 tablespoons shortening

1 large onion, chopped

2 cloves garlic, chopped

½ pound ham, diced ½ inch thick

2 teaspoons salt

1 teaspoon freshly ground black pepper

6 cups hot fluffy cooked white rice

1. Put the soaked white beans in a heavy bean pot and add the water. Bring to a simmer and cover.

2. In a skillet, render the fat from the bacon and brown the chopped onion, garlic, and ham. Add to the beans.

3. Simmer for 1½ to 2 hours, until the beans are tender. Season with salt and pepper.

4. Continue cooking until the beans are quite tender and the liquid in the pot is thick. If the liquid evaporates before the beans are completely tender add more water.

5. Serve with hot white rice.

. . . .

Notes and Variations

Other seasoning meats such as pickled pork or pork sausage can be used in place of the ham. Or meat can be left out all together for a no-meat entree. Use another rice such as brown, popcorn, or basmati. Eliminating the ham, bacon, and salt reduces the analysis to 383 calories, less than 1 gram fat, 0 mg cholesterol, and only 24 mg sodium.

NUTRITIONAL ANALYSIS

Calories:	488	
Protein:	27	g
Carbohydrates:	74	g
Dietary Fiber:	12	g
Fat:	9.5	g
Cholesterol:	23	mg
Sodium:	1226	mg

Percent of Calories

Protein:	22 %
Carbohydrates:	60 %
Fat:	18 %

AMERICAN WHITE BEAN SOUP

Serves 8

1 *pound white beans, soaked*
10 *cups water*
1 *smoked ham hock*
2 *bay leaves*
1 *large potato, diced*
2 *medium white onions, chopped*
2 *ribs celery, chopped*
4 *cloves garlic, minced*
2 *teaspoons salt*
1 *teaspoon white pepper*
¼ *cup chopped parsley*

1. Simmer the beans in the water with the ham hock and bay leaves until tender, about 1½ hours.

2. Add the potato, onions, celery, and garlic. Season with salt and white pepper. Simmer for another hour, until the beans are breaking apart. Add more water during cooking if the liquid becomes too thick. Remove the bay leaves.

3. Transfer the ham hock to a plate and remove the meat. Dice the meat and discard the bones. Return the meat to the beans.

4. Allow the soup to cool somewhat and perform this next step with great care. Ladle the beans into a blender container, only enough to fill half the container. Cover carefully and puree the beans until thoroughly smooth. Pour the puree into a bowl and repeat this step until all the beans are processed. Pour the beans back into the pot, reheat, and adjust the seasonings if desired.

5. Fold in the chopped parsley and serve.

. . . .

Notes and Variations

This is a simple recipe that can be changed to suit your taste. The beans don't have to be pureed, but can simply be cooked longer and then stirred forcefully with a wooden spoon or even a whisk to break up the beans into a smoother soup consistency. The ham hock is not necessary if you prefer a vegetarian rendition. Most of the fat and cholesterol has been cooked out of the ham hock in the smoking, so it adds a great deal of flavor without adding excessive fat or cholesterol.

NUTRITIONAL ANALYSIS

Calories:	255
Protein:	14.9 g
Carbohydrates:	45 g
Dietary Fiber:	11.9 g
Fat:	2.2 g
Cholesterol:	6.9 mg
Sodium:	573 mg

Percent of Calories

Protein:	23 %
Carbohydrates:	69 %
Fat:	8 %

WHITE BEAN PUREE WITH ONIONS

Serves 6 as a side

1 *pound white beans, soaked*
8 *cups water*
3 *large onions, chopped*
1 *tablespoon rosemary*
2 *cloves garlic, chopped*
2 *teaspoons salt*
1 *teaspoon white pepper*

. . . .

1. Simmer the beans in the water for 1½ hours, until tender.

2. Add the onions, rosemary, and garlic.

3. Season with salt and white pepper.

4. Simmer, uncovered, until the beans are very tender. Roughly stir the beans around in the pot to break them up into a mash. If the mash is too loose, continue simmering to dry out a bit more.

. . . .

Notes and Variations

Season with chopped fresh herbs to serve if desired, or add some butter or heavy cream. Use this as you would rice or mashed potatoes. Try red beans in white bean puree. Use instead of rice.
Try this with meat loaf instead of rice or potatoes.

NUTRITIONAL ANALYSIS

Calories:	269	
Protein:	16.5	g
Carbohydrates:	50	g
Dietary Fiber:	14.5	g
Fat:	1	g
Cholesterol:	0	mg
Sodium:	727	mg

Percent of Calories

Protein:	24%
Carbohydrates:	72%
Fat:	4%

BOSTON BAKED BEANS

Serves 6 as a side

1   *pound small white haricot beans, soaked*
8   *cups water*
1   *medium onion, minced*
¼   *cup molasses*
¼   *cup brown sugar*
1   *tablespoon dry mustard*
2   *teaspoons salt*
4   *ounces salt pork*

1. Combine the beans and water in a soup pot and simmer, covered, for 1½ hours, until the beans begin to tenderize. Drain the beans, reserving the liquid.

2. Combine the beans with the minced onion, molasses, brown sugar, mustard, and salt. Transfer to a covered, ovenproof baking dish.

3. Slice up the salt pork into 6 pieces and place over the top of the beans. Cover the dish and place in a preheated 350°F oven and bake for 1 hour.

4. Remove the dish from the oven. Stir in 1 to 2 cups of the reserved cooking liquid (enough to add liquid if the beans are drying out), cover, and return to the oven. Bake for another hour.

5. Serve if beans are baked to your preference or bake longer.

Notes and Variations

The beans should be carefully stirred several times during the baking. The finished beans should have a nice, rich brown color. Some recipes contain catsup as an ingredient — use about ¼ cup if you wish. For sweeter beans, add more molasses, brown sugar, or both. The reserved cooking liquor can be added as needed, even just before serving, if desired.

Lighter Version

Omit the salt and salt pork.
Use only half the measures for molasses and brown sugar.

NUTRITIONAL ANALYSIS

	Regular		Lighter Version	
Calories:	457		303	
Protein:	21	g	17	g
Carbohydrates:	65	g	57	g
Dietary Fiber:	15	g	14.5	g
Fat:	13.5	g	1.5	g
Cholesterol:	17	mg	0	mg
Sodium:	989	mg	23	mg

Percent of Calories

	Regular	Lighter Version
Protein:	18%	22%
Carbohydrates:	56%	73%
Fat:	26%	5%

CATALAN WHITE HARICOT BEANS WITH DUCKLING

Serves 6 as an entree

1 pound dried white haricot beans, soaked
8 cups water
1 6-pound duckling, cut into pieces as for frying
2 teaspoons salt
2 teaspoons black pepper
1 cup all-purpose flour
2 tablespoons olive oil
12 strips bacon
3 medium onions, chopped
1 cup dry red wine
1 cup duck or chicken stock
2 tablespoons tomato paste
½ cup pine nuts
2 cloves garlic, minced
2 bay leaves
1 teaspoon dried thyme leaves
1 teaspoon dried oregano leaves
¼ cup chopped parsley

1. Combine the soaked white haricot beans and water, bring to a simmer, cover, and cook for 1½ hours, until the beans are tender.

2. While the beans are cooking, prepare the duck. Salt and pepper the duck pieces and dredge them in flour. Put aside.

3. Heat the olive oil in a Dutch oven and sauté the bacon until crisp. Transfer the bacon to a plate and crumble when cool enough to handle.

4. Brown the prepared duck pieces on all sides in the remaining oil and bacon drippings.

5. Add the chopped onions to the remaining bacon drippings and sauté until browned lightly.

6. Add the beans, red wine, stock, tomato paste, pine nuts, garlic, bay leaves, thyme, and oregano. Bring to a simmer and cover. Transfer the Dutch oven to a 375°F oven and cook for 1 hour, until the duck pieces are tender. Remove the bay leaves.

7. Crumble the cooked bacon and sprinkle it and the parsley over the beans before serving.

. . . .

Notes and Variations

I use a cleaver to hack the duck into smaller pieces so more pieces can go into each serving. Each breast half can be cut into 3 pieces, each thigh into 2 pieces. With the legs left whole this gives you 12 pieces to serve 6, 2 pieces each. Though duck is nice, a large baking hen, capon, or goose can be used here. There should not be too much liquid remaining when the dish is served. However, if the beans become too dry during cooking, add more stock or water.

. . . .

Lighter Version

Omit the olive oil, bacon, and salt. Remove and discard the duck skin. Cook the seasoned and flour-dredged duck pieces in a hot pan with no fat or liquid. Move the pieces so they don't stick and burn. This takes some added attention to the pot but eliminates the need for oil and fat. Replace the chicken stock with a low-fat stock or broth. Increase the garlic measure by 4 cloves and double the measure of bay leaves, thyme, and oregano.

NUTRITIONAL ANALYSIS

	Regular		Lighter Version	
Calories:	1772		624	
Protein:	54	g	41	g
Carbohydrates:	73	g	73	g
Dietary Fiber:	3	g	3	g
Fat:	138	g	17	g
Cholesterol:	230	mg	79	mg
Sodium:	1428	mg	155	mg

Percent of Calories

Protein:	12%	26%
Carbohydrates:	16%	46%
Fat:	70%	24%

AUSTRIAN GOOSE DRUMSTICKS WITH BARLEY AND WHITE BEANS *Serves 6 as an entree*

  1   *pound dried white haricot beans, soaked*
  8   *cups water*
  1   *cup uncooked pearl barley*
  3   *goose drumsticks*
  1   *large onion, large dice*
  1   *kohlrabi, large dice*
  2   *medium carrots, large dice*
  2   *medium turnips, large dice*
  3   *cloves garlic, pressed*
  ½   *cup lard (traditional) or oil*
  1   *tablespoon paprika*
  2   *teaspoons salt*
  1   *teaspoon black pepper*

1. Bring the beans and water to a simmer in an ovenproof casserole or Dutch oven. Cover and simmer for ½ hour.

2. Add the dried barley, goose drumsticks, onion, kohlrabi, carrots, turnips, garlic, and lard. Season with paprika, salt, and pepper. Fold all together well and cover and place in a preheated 350°F oven for 3 hours. Check periodically and add additional water if desired.

3. Check to see if the beans, barley, and drumsticks are tender. If not, continue cooking for another hour, adding additional water if necessary.

4. To serve, remove and discard the bones from the drumsticks and split the meat of each into 2 servings. Serve with the rest of the dish.

. . . .

Notes and Variations

Turkey drumsticks can be used in place of goose drumsticks. Try smoked turkey or smoked goose drumsticks if available. And there's no reason why you can't simply use a whole chicken. Take it out when it is cooked and remove the bones. Parsnips can be used in place of the turnips. Cabbage can be used in place of the kohlrabi. Butter or olive oil can be used in place of the lard.

. . . .

Lighter Version

Omit the lard and salt. Remove and discard the skin and fat from the drumsticks. Add 1 more tablespoon paprika.

NUTRITIONAL ANALYSIS

	Regular		Lighter Version	
Calories:	904		587	
Protein:	48.5	g	41.5	g
Carbohydrates:	85	g	85.5	g
Dietary Fiber:	23	g	23	g
Fat:	42	g	10.5	g
Cholesterol:	114	mg	66	mg
Sodium:	863	mg	129	mg

Percent of Calories

Protein:	21%	27%
Carbohydrates:	37%	57%
Fat:	42%	16%

HAMBURG-STYLE WHITE BEANS WITH PEARS AND BACON

Serves 6 as an entree

2 tablespoons butter

1 pound smoked slab bacon, cut into ½-inch dice

8 cups water

1 pound dried white beans

3 large pears

1 teaspoon salt

1 teaspoon white pepper

. . . .

1. Melt the butter in a soup pot and sauté the diced bacon until it browns lightly.

2. Add the water and beans. Cover and simmer for 1½ hours, until the beans are tender enough to serve.

3. Core and dice the pears and add to the beans. Season with salt and white pepper.

4. Simmer for 15 minutes more and serve.

. . . .

Notes and Variations

Diced smoked sliced bacon or Canadian bacon can be used as well as slab bacon.
Apples can replace the pears. Salt carefully; there is salt in the bacon.

. . . .

Lighter Version

*Omit the butter and salt. Replace the
slab bacon with a cooked low-fat bacon
or a cooked lean Canadian bacon.*

NUTRITIONAL ANALYSIS

	Regular		Lighter Version	
Calories:	650		392	
Protein:	24	g	28	g
Carbohydrates:	60	g	60.5	g
Dietary Fiber:	16.5	g	16.5	g
Fat:	36	g	5	g
Cholesterol:	51	mg	27	mg
Sodium:	914	mg	755	mg

Percent of Calories

Protein:	15 %	28 %
Carbohydrates:	36 %	60 %
Fat:	49 %	12 %

PORTO WHITE HARICOT BEANS AND TRIPE

Serves 6 as an entree

1	pound dried white haricot beans, soaked
10	cups water
1	split calf's foot or pig's foot
2	pounds tripe, cut into 1-inch squares
½	cup lard (traditional) or olive oil
2	large yellow onions, finely chopped
2	large carrots, scrubbed and sliced
4	cloves garlic, chopped
½	pound chorizo sausages, sliced
½	pound smoked ham, cut into ½-inch dice
2	bay leaves
1	teaspoon ground cumin
1	tablespoon paprika
¼	cup chopped parsley
2	teaspoons salt
1	teaspoon black or white pepper

1. Drain the white haricot beans and combine with the water in a soup pot. Add the split calf's or pig's foot and the tripe. Bring to a simmer and cook for 1½ hours, until the beans begin to tenderize and the meat is tender. Remove the meat pieces to a plate or cutting board. Remove and discard the bones. Cut the meat into ½-inch dice. Return the diced meat to the beans and tripe. Cover and continue simmering gently.

2. In a sauté pan, heat the olive oil or lard and sauté the chopped onions and carrots until the onions soften. Add the garlic, chorizo, ham, and bay leaves. Sauté together until the vegetables begin to color. Remove the bay leaves. Transfer to the soup pot.

3. Add the cumin, paprika, and chopped parsley. Season to taste with salt and pepper. Simmer for 30 minutes more and serve.

Notes and Variations

When chorizo sausages are not available freshly made, they can usually be found canned in specialty food stores that carry Spanish products. A prosciutto-type ham can be used in place of the smoked ham. If used, be careful in the additional salting of the dish. Tomatoes can also be added to this dish. Dice 2 large ripe tomatoes and add to the sauté pan with the onions and other ingredients.

Lighter Version

Omit the olive oil and salt. Omit the pig's foot and add 2 packets dry unflavored gelatin when the sautéed seasoning vegetables and meats are added. This will add the natural gelatin that would have come from the pig's foot, which helps add a silken texture and additional density to the dish. The chorizo sausages and the ham can be replaced with the same measure of low-fat, low-sodium sausage and ham. Add 4 more garlic cloves and 2 more bay leaves.

NUTRITIONAL ANALYSIS

	Regular		Lighter Version	
Calories:	859		528	
Protein:	57	g	53.4	g
Carbohydrates:	56	g	57	g
Dietary Fiber:	15.7	g	15.7	g
Fat:	45.3	g	9.7	g
Cholesterol:	220	mg	177	mg
Sodium:	1631	mg	607	mg

Percent of Calories

Protein:	26%	40%
Carbohydrates:	26%	43%
Fat:	48%	17%

Riojan White Beans with Quail

Serves 6 as an entree

1   pound dried white haricot beans, presoaked and drained
8   cups water
4   tablespoons lard or olive oil
6   dressed quail
    Salt and pepper to season quail
½   pound ham, diced
4   chorizo sausages, sliced into rounds
2   medium onions, chopped
4   cloves garlic, chopped
4   medium tomatoes, skinned, seeded, and chopped
2   bay leaves
1   tablespoon chopped fresh oregano
2   teaspoons salt
1   teaspoon black pepper

1. Rinse the soaked white beans and put them in a pot with the water. Bring to a simmer, cover, and cook for 1½ hours, until the beans become somewhat tender.

2. Heat the lard or olive oil in a skillet or sauté pan. Season the quail with salt and pepper and sauté in the hot fat, on all sides, until thoroughly cooked. Remove the cooked quail from the pan and set aside.

3. Add the ham, chorizo, and chopped onions to the remaining fat in the pan and sauté until the onions begin to color.

4. Add the garlic and tomatoes, bay leaves, and oregano. Simmer until the sauce begins to thicken.

5. When the beans are tender, remove the cover from the pot and simmer off any cooking liquid standing above the top of the beans.

6. Carefully fold in the tomato sauce. Season with salt and pepper.

7. Add the quail, cover and simmer for another 30 minutes, until the quail is tender. Remove the bay leaves.

8. Serve into bowls with 1 quail per serving on top.

. . . .

Notes and Variations

The more readily available Cornish hen can replace the quail — use 3 halved Cornish hens. Use an available smoked sausage in place of the chorizo if you wish. Use 1 teaspoon dried oregano in place of the 1 tablespoon fresh.

. . . .

Lighter Version

Omit the lard or olive oil and salt. Skin the quail before preparation. Cook the pepper-seasoned skinless quail in a dry pan, moving regularly to prevent sticking and burning. Replace the ham and chorizo with low-fat ham and sausage, perhaps turkey products. Add 2 more bay leaves and another tablespoon chopped fresh oregano.

NUTRITIONAL ANALYSIS

	Regular		Lighter Version	
Calories:	806		484	
Protein:	57	g	51	g
Carbohydrates:	55.5	g	56	g
Dietary Fiber:	16	g	16	g
Fat:	39.5	g	7	g
Cholesterol:	145	mg	98	mg
Sodium:	2119	mg	987	mg

Percent of Calories

Protein:	28%	41%
Carbohydrates:	28%	45%
Fat:	44%	13%

WHITE BEANS AND LAMB WITH HERBS

Serves 6 as an entree

  1 *pound dried white haricot beans, presoaked*
  8 *cups water*
  3 *tablespoons olive oil*
  1 *pound lean lamb, small dice*
  2 *medium onions, chopped*
  4 *cloves garlic, chopped*
  ½ *cup Madeira wine*
  2 *teaspoons salt*
  1 *teaspoon white pepper*
  1 *large tomato, small dice*
  2 *teaspoons minced fresh rosemary leaves*
  2 *teaspoons chopped fresh thyme*
 4½ *cups hot fluffy cooked rice*
  3 *tablespoons chopped parsley*
  1 *tablespoon chopped fresh mint leaves*

1. In a bean pot, combine the dried white haricot beans with the water, cover and simmer for 1½ hours, until the beans become somewhat tender.

2. In a sauté pan, heat the olive oil and sauté the diced lamb until it browns. Add the chopped onions and garlic and continue cooking until lightly browned. Add the Madeira and boil for 2 minutes. Add to the bean pot. Season to taste with salt and white pepper. Simmer for another ½ hour, until the beans are ready to serve.

3. Add the diced tomato, minced rosemary, and chopped thyme and cook for 5 minutes more.

4. Just before serving on the hot fluffy rice, add the parsley and mint to the beans.

. . . .

Notes and Variations

The lamb can be ground. If using dried herbs, use only one third measure of the fresh.
The rice can be white, brown, Arborio, or jasmine — your choice.

. . . .

Lighter Version

*Omit the olive oil and salt. Use very lean
lamb and reduce the measure to
½ pound. Add an additional teaspoon
each of rosemary and thyme.*

NUTRITIONAL ANALYSIS

	Regular		Lighter Version	
Calories:	712		567	
Protein:	33	g	28.6	g
Carbohydrates:	98	g	98	g
Dietary Fiber:	16.6	g	16.6	g
Fat:	18.6	g	4.3	g
Cholesterol:	47.3	mg	24.3	mg
Sodium:	540	mg	47	mg

Percent of Calories

Protein:	18 %	20 %
Carbohydrates:	55 %	69 %
Fat:	24 %	7 %

HUNGARIAN WHITE BEANS WITH SLAB BACON

Serves 6 as an entree

- 1 pound dried white haricot beans
- 8 cups water
- ½ pound lean smoked slab bacon
- 2 bay leaves
- 2 tablespoons olive oil
- 1 tablespoon flour
- 1 medium onion, chopped
- 2 cloves garlic, minced
- 1 tablespoon cider vinegar
- 2 teaspoons sugar
- ½ cup sour cream
- 2 teaspoons salt

1. In a bean pot, combine the beans with the water. Cut the slab bacon into two pieces: one-third and two-thirds. Add the two-thirds piece to the beans and water, along with the bay leaves, and bring to a simmer. Cover and cook for 1½ hours, until the beans are tender. Remove the bay leaves.

2. Mince the remaining one-third of the bacon and sauté briefly in a sauté pan with the olive oil. Add the flour, onion, and garlic and cook together for 2 minutes. Add some of the liquid from the bean pot and blend the flour and the ingredients together. Return the mixture to the bean pot. Cover and continue cooking until the beans are tender enough for serving.

3. Add the vinegar, sugar, and sour cream. Season to taste with salt.

4. Remove the two-thirds bacon piece to a plate or cutting board and slice it into 6 pieces. Add it to the beans and simmer for 5 minutes.

5. Serve the beans with a piece of bacon on top.

. . . .

Notes and Variations

The better the bacon, the better the resulting dish. Corned beef brisket can be used in place of the bacon. A wine or distilled vinegar can be used as well as a flavored vinegar such as raspberry. More sour cream can be added if you prefer.

. . . .

Lighter Version

Omit the olive oil and salt. Replace the slab bacon with a lean cooked Canadian bacon. Cook the one-third piece Canadian bacon, minced, dry with the other ingredients in the sauté pan. Stir constantly for about 5 minutes to cook without burning. Replace the sour cream with nonfat sour cream.

NUTRITIONAL ANALYSIS

	Regular		Lighter Version	
Calories:	574		358	
Protein:	22.5	g	26.5	g
Carbohydrates:	51	g	54	g
Dietary Fiber:	14.5	g	14.5	g
Fat:	30	g	4	g
Cholesterol:	46	mg	23	mg
Sodium:	1500	mg	1329	mg

Percent of Calories

Protein:	16 %	30 %
Carbohydrates:	36 %	60 %
Fat:	48 %	10 %

CANNELLINI WITH ITALIAN SAUSAGE

Serves 6

1 *pound dried cannellini beans, soaked overnight*
3 *tablespoons light flavored olive oil*
6 *Italian sausages*
2 *medium yellow onions, peeled and chopped*
6 *cloves garlic, peeled and chopped*
2 *ribs celery, stringed and chopped*
1 *large sweet red or green bell pepper, stemmed, seeded, and chopped*
1 *teaspoon aniseed*
1 *teaspoon dried oregano leaves*
1 *teaspoon dried rosemary leaves*
1 *teaspoon crushed dried hot red pepper*
1½ *quarts water*
2 *teaspoons salt or to taste*
¼ *cup chopped parsley*

1. Soak the white haricot beans overnight or quick-soak. Pour off the soaking water, rinse the beans, and set aside.

2. Add the olive oil to a bean pot and heat. Add the Italian sausages and sauté until nicely browned. Pierce the sausages several times with the tip of a knife or fork to release the fat and flavor into the cooking liquid.

3. Add the onions, garlic, celery, and bell pepper. Sauté until the vegetables begin to color. Add the aniseed, oregano, rosemary, and dried hot red pepper. Add the water and beans.

4. Bring to a simmer and cook for 1 hour. Test the beans for tenderness and add the salt. If needed, continue simmering the beans until they are of the desired tenderness.

5. Adjust the seasonings, if desired, and stir in the chopped parsley.

6. Serve in bowls with 1 Italian sausage on the top of each serving.

· ·

Notes and Variations

Any dried white haricot bean will work here: navy or great Northern. If you do not want the heat of the red pepper, substitute black pepper to taste. The Italian sausages can be cut into pieces the size of your choice, rather than left whole. I prefer it cut into half-inch rounds so that more of the sausage flavor is infused into the whole dish. This recipe can be served over rice.

· ·

Lighter Version

Omit the olive oil, Italian sausages, and salt. Add 1 onion, 1 bell pepper, 2 garlic cloves, 1 teaspoon anise seeds, and ¼ cup chopped parsley.

NUTRITIONAL ANALYSIS

	Regular		Lighter Version	
Calories:	605		296	
Protein:	28	g	17	g
Carbohydrates:	54	g	56	g
Dietary fiber:	16	g	17	g
Fat:	32	g	1	g
Cholesterol:	58	mg	0	mg
Sodium:	1295	mg	32	mg

Percent of Calories

Protein:	18%	23%
Carbohydrates:	35%	73%
Fat:	47%	4%

BÉARNAISE OUILLAT SOUP

Serves 10

1 *pound dried white beans, soaked overnight*

12 *cups water*

6 *tablespoons butter*

4 *large onions, thinly sliced*

10 *cloves garlic, chopped*

2 *ribs celery, chopped*

2 *tablespoons chopped parsley*

1 *teaspoon dried thyme*

2 *bay leaves*

2 *teaspoons salt*

1 *teaspoon freshly ground white pepper*

2 *cups grated Emmenthaler cheese*

1. In a large bean pot, combine the soaked white haricot beans and water, cover, and simmer for 2½ hours. The beans should be beginning to break apart at this point.

2. In a separate sauté pan, melt the butter and sauté the sliced onions, chopped garlic, and chopped celery until browned lightly. Add to the bean pot.

3. Add the parsley, thyme, bay leaves, and season to taste with salt and white pepper. Simmer for another ½ hour, stirring roughly to break apart the white beans, allowing to make a thick soup of the liquid. Discard the bay leaves.

4. To serve, ladle the soup into bowls and sprinkle generously with the grated cheese.

. . . .

Notes and Variations

This soup is a specialty of the city of Bearn, France. It is named after the pot in which it is cooked, the "ouille." This soup is also made with fava beans or other haricot beans. Gruyère or another Swiss-type cheese can be used in place of the Emmenthaler.

. . . .

Lighter Version

Omit the butter and salt. Replace the Emmenthaler with a low-fat Swiss cheese. Add another teaspoon thyme and 2 more bay leaves.

NUTRITIONAL ANALYSIS

	Regular		Lighter Version	
Calories:	343		231	
Protein:	18	g	18	g
Carbohydrates:	36	g	36.5	g
Dietary Fiber:	10	g	10	g
Fat:	15	g	2	g
Cholesterol:	43	mg	10	mg
Sodium:	580	mg	415	mg

Percent of Calories

Protein:	21%	30%
Carbohydrates:	41%	62%
Fat:	38%	8%

CATALAN BACALAO AND WHITE BEAN SALAD

Serves 6 as an entree salad

- 1 pound white haricot beans, soaked overnight
- 10 cups water
- 1 pound bacalao (salt cod), soaked overnight in cool running tap water
- 1 large onion, chopped
- 2 medium tomatoes, diced
- 3 dozen oil-cured black olives
- 4 hard-boiled eggs, chopped
- ¼ cup chopped parsley
- 1 cup olive oil
- ⅓ cup red wine vinegar
- 2 teaspoons salt
- 1 teaspoon freshly ground black pepper

1. Simmer the beans in the water for an hour or so, until tender but not too soft. Drain and refrigerate.

2. In a saucepan or skillet, combine the bacalao with enough water to cover, bring the water to a gentle simmer, and cook for about 20 minutes, until the bacalao becomes tender. Remove the bacalao from the water, flake into rough pieces, and refrigerate.

3. In a bowl, combine the cooked white beans and the cooked flaked bacalao with the chopped onion, diced tomatoes, black olives, chopped hard-boiled eggs, and chopped parsley. Stir in the olive oil, red wine vinegar, and season to taste with salt and freshly ground black pepper.

4. Cover the bowl and refrigerate until cold before serving.

Notes and Variations

Any haricot will work. Fresh cod can be used in place of the salt cod and a good quality canned tuna can also be used.

Lighter Version

Omit the olive oil and salt. Replace the oil-cured olives with water-packed olives. Replace the 4 whole hard-boiled eggs with 8 hard-boiled egg whites. Add 2 cloves pressed garlic.

NUTRITIONAL ANALYSIS

	Regular		Lighter Version	
Calories:	935		537	
Protein:	70	g	71	g
Carbohydrates:	55.5	g	53	g
Dietary Fiber:	13	g	13	g
Fat:	47.5	g	4.5	g
Cholesterol:	256	mg	115	mg
Sodium:	2192	mg	1956	mg

Percent of Calories

Protein:	30%		53%	
Carbohydrates:	24%		40%	
Fat:	46%		8%	

GREEK CANNELLINI

Serves 6 as an entree

1   pound dried cannellini, navy, or great Northerns,
    soaked overnight or quick-soaked
8   cups water, or more if needed
2   large tomatoes, skinned, seeded, and chopped
2   ribs celery, finely chopped
1   large onion, finely chopped
1   large carrot, finely diced
2   tablespoons tomato paste
¼   cup chopped parsley
⅓   cup green fruity olive oil
2   teaspoons salt or to taste
1   teaspoon freshly ground black pepper
1   teaspoon sugar
6   parsley sprigs for garnish

1. Combine the beans and water in a bean pot and bring to a simmer.
2. Add the chopped tomatoes, celery, onion, and carrot.
3. Stir in the tomato paste, chopped parsley, and olive oil.
4. Season with salt, black pepper, and sugar.
5. Cover and simmer for 2 hours, stirring carefully, on occasion, during the cooking.
6. Check the beans for tenderness and adjust the seasonings as desired.
7. Serve garnished with parsley sprigs.

Notes and Variations

I normally don't bother with skinning and seeding the tomatoes — it's up to you. The celery can include the leaves. If the beans are not tender enough after 2 hours of cooking, cook for another 30 minutes, until they are tender. Different beans have different cooking times.

Lighter Version

Omit the olive oil and salt. Increase the pepper by 1 teaspoon. Add 2 tablespoons lemon juice with the other ingredients.

NUTRITIONAL ANALYSIS

	Regular		Lighter Version	
Calories:	1219		591	
Protein:	26.5	g	26.5	g
Carbohydrates:	115.5	g	118	g
Dietary Fiber:	29	g	29	g
Fat:	75.6	g	3.7	g
Cholesterol:			0	mg
Sodium:	5381	mg	1118	mg

Percent of Calories

Protein:	8%	17%
Carbohydrates:	37%	77%
Fat:	55%	5%

HUNGARIAN WHITE BEAN GOULASH

Serves 6 as an entree

1   *pound dried white haricot beans, soaked overnight or quick-soaked*

8   *cups water*

2   *teaspoons salt*

1½   *pounds unpeeled potatoes, scrubbed and cut into ¾-inch dice*

4   *tablespoons lard (traditional) or oil*

2   *medium onions, chopped*

2   *sweet green bell peppers, seeded and thinly sliced*

6   *cloves garlic, minced*

2   *teaspoons caraway seeds*

1   *large tomato, diced*

3   *tablespoons Hungarian paprika, preferably hot*

1. In a bean pot, simmer the soaked beans covered in the water until tender, but not soft, about 1½ hours. Add more water if necessary during the cooking.

2. Season with salt and add the diced potatoes. Cook for another 30 minutes.

3. While the potatoes and beans are finishing their cooking, heat the lard or fat in a large sauté pan and add the chopped onions, bell peppers, garlic, and caraway seeds. Sauté until the vegetables begin to color and add to the bean pot. Add the tomato and paprika to the pot.

4. Simmer gently for 20 minutes, adjust seasonings if desired, and serve in bowls.

Notes and Variations

The measure of paprika can be reduced if it becomes too hot. Freshly bought, good-quality paprika makes all the difference in this recipe. Do try to use Hungarian paprika. It is generally more flavorful than what is packed by most spice companies. A flat paprika will produce a flat dish. As always, watch the beans simmering time to be certain that they do not become too soft in the cooking. Fold the cooked vegetables gently into the beans without breaking up the potatoes.

Lighter Version

Omit the salt and lard. Increase the measures of garlic by 2 cloves, caraway seeds by 1 teaspoon, and paprika by 1 tablespoon, provided the paprika is not too hot. Add 2 tablespoons cider vinegar when the cooked vegetables are added to the pot.

NUTRITIONAL ANALYSIS

	Regular		Lighter Version	
Calories:	459		389	
Protein:	19.5	g	20	g
Carbohydrates:	76	g	77	g
Dietary Fiber:	18.5	g	19	g
Fat:	10.3	g	2	g
Cholesterol:	8.1	mg	0	mg
Sodium:	739	mg	29	mg

Percent of Calories

Protein:	16 %	19 %
Carbohydrates:	64 %	76 %
Fat:	20 %	4 %

SERBIAN WHITE BEAN SOUP

Serves 8

1 *pound dried white beans, soaked overnight*
10 *cups unsalted rich veal or beef stock*
4 *tablespoons lard*
2 *medium onions, chopped*
2 *medium turnips, scrubbed and diced*
4 *tablespoons flour*
6 *garlic cloves, chopped*
2 *teaspoons salt or to taste*
1 *teaspoon freshly ground black pepper*
2 *tablespoons hot paprika*
2 *cups yogurt*
2 *teaspoons white vinegar*

1. In a large saucepan or bean pot, combine the soaked white beans with the veal or beef stock. Bring to a gentle simmer, cover and cook for 2½ hours, until the beans are beginning to thicken the cooking liquid.

2. In a sauté pan, melt the lard and sauté the chopped onions and diced turnips until they begin to color. Stir in the flour and continue cooking for 5 minutes more, and continue to scrape the flour from the pan to prevent any burning.

3. Add the chopped garlic to the sauté pan vegetables and ladle about 1 cup of the soup liquid into the pan. Bring to a boil to deglaze the pan, scraping well any flour from the pan bottom. Add the mixture to the soup pot. Season to taste with salt and freshly ground black pepper.

4. Add the hot paprika, yogurt, and vinegar. Heat for 1 minute more without bringing to a boil.

5. Serve immediately.

. . . .

Notes and Variations

Any haricot bean works well in this recipe. Try it with black beans or pinto beans. The stock is unsalted because if the beans are cooked with salted liquid from the start they will remain hard from the salt and require a much longer cooking time. The stock can be chicken instead of veal or beef — your preference as long as it is unsalted. Butter or oil can replace the lard if you wish. Do not simmer or boil the beans after the yogurt has been added or it will curdle.

. . . .

Lighter Version

Omit the lard and salt. Use a nonfat, low-sodium stock. Instead of sautéing the vegetables in the lard and adding the flour, whisk the flour directly into the bean pot after the beans have simmered for 1½ hours. Also, add the onions, turnips, and garlic directly to the beans at this point. Season with salt and pepper. Cover and simmer gently for another hour. Replace the plain whole milk yogurt with nonfat yogurt. Do not simmer or boil the beans after the yogurt is added or it will curdle. Add an additional teaspoon vinegar.

NUTRITIONAL ANALYSIS

	Regular		Lighter Version	
Calories:	391		351	
Protein:	22	g	29	g
Carbohydrates:	52.5	g	54	g
Dietary Fiber:	13	g	13	g
Fat:	11.5	g	3	g
Cholesterol:	14	mg	1	mg
Sodium:	677	mg	244	mg

Percent of Calories

Protein:	22 %		32 %	
Carbohydrates:	52 %		60 %	
Fat:	25 %		8 %	

ROMANESQUE WHITE BEAN SOUP *Serves 8*

1 *pound dried white beans, soaked overnight*
10 *cups water*
2 *tablespoons lard*
½ *pound salt pork, finely chopped*
2 *large onions, finely chopped*
4 *cloves garlic, minced*
2 *ribs celery, minced*
2 *large tomatoes, skinned, seeded, and chopped*
2 *teaspoons salt*
1 *teaspoon freshly ground black pepper*
2 *cups small elbow macaroni*
½ *cup grated Romano cheese*

1. In a bean pot or large saucepan, combine the soaked white beans and water, cover, and simmer for 2 hours.

2. In a sauté pan, heat the lard and sauté the chopped salt pork, chopped onions, and minced garlic and celery until browned lightly.

3. Add the chopped tomatoes and the cooked vegetables to the bean pot. Season to taste with salt and freshly ground black pepper. Simmer together for 10 minutes.

4. Ten minutes before serving, add the elbow macaroni and simmer until the pasta is cooked al dente. Stir in the Romano cheese and serve immediately.

. . . .

Notes and Variations

This is a simple but very delicious soup. The lard can be replaced with olive oil. Fresh Roma tomatoes are nice in place of the regular tomatoes, and they really don't need to be skinned and seeded. Another pasta of your preference can be used in place of the small elbow macaroni — small penne or broken vermicelli. The Romano cheese can be replaced with Parmesan or a mix of both. Put more grated cheese and a peppermill on the table for your guests.

. . . .

Lighter Version

Omit the lard and salt. Instead of sautéing the seasoning vegetables in the lard, add directly to the beans after the beans have cooked for 1½ hours. Reduce the measure of salt pork from ½ to ¼ pound. Replace the Romano cheese with a nonfat Parmesan cheese; Parmesan and Romano cheese are two of the lowest fat cheeses. If used sparingly, they will not add too much fat. Add 2 cloves garlic.

NUTRITIONAL ANALYSIS

	Regular		*Lighter Version*	
Calories:	326		282	
Protein:	19.5	g	17	g
Carbohydrates:	49	g	51	g
Dietary Fiber:	10	g	10	g
Fat:	6	g	1.5	g
Cholesterol:	19.5	mg	10	mg
Sodium:	1061	mg	226	mg

Percent of Calories

Protein:	24 %	24 %
Carbohydrates:	59 %	71 %
Fat:	17 %	5 %

TUSCAN-STYLE WHITE BEANS   *Serves 8 as a side*

1   *pound white beans*
¼   *cup fruity green olive oil*
1   *teaspoon sage*
4   *cloves garlic, sliced*
8   *cups water, or more*
2   *large fresh tomatoes, peeled and diced*
2   *teaspoons salt*
1   *teaspoon freshly ground white pepper*
2   *tablespoons olive oil*

1. Rinse and pick over the beans. Soak overnight or quick-soak.

2. Combine the beans, olive oil, sage, garlic, and water in a bean pot. Bring to a simmer, cover, and cook for 2 hours, until the beans are tender. Add the tomatoes and simmer for 10 minutes more.

3. Season with salt, white pepper, and the additional olive oil and serve in bowls.

Notes and Variations

The simple addition of fresh herbs added just before serving greatly enhances this recipe. Try 2 tablespoons thyme, oregano, basil, or ¼ cup chopped parsley. The tomatoes can be added at the end of cooking if you want to see tomato pieces. Any haricot bean — red, white, or black — can be used in this recipe. Serve over rice as an entree. Try Arborio or brown rice.

. . . .

Lighter Version

Omit the olive oil and salt.
Add 1 teaspoon sage, 2 cloves garlic,
1 tomato, and ½ teaspoon white pepper.
Finish with 2 tablespoons chopped
parsley.

NUTRITIONAL ANALYSIS

	Regular	*Lighter Version*
Calories:	143	59
Protein:	2.6 g	2.8 g
Carbohydrates:	10 g	11.2 g
Dietary Fiber:	2.6 g	2.8 g
Fat:	10.5 g	<.5 g
Cholesterol:	0 mg	0 mg
Sodium:	654 mg	123 mg

Percent of Calories

Protein:	7 %	19 %
Carbohydrates:	28 %	75 %
Fat:	65 %	6 %

TURKISH WHITE BEAN STEW *Serves 6 as an entree*

1 *pound dried white navy beans, soaked overnight*
10 *cups water*
½ *cup olive oil*
4 *medium onions, chopped*
4 *ribs celery, chopped*
2 *large carrots, diced*
2 *cloves garlic, chopped*
6 *tablespoons tomato paste*
¼ *cup freshly squeezed lemon juice*
1 *teaspoon sugar*
½ *teaspoon cayenne pepper*
2 *teaspoons salt*
½ *cup chopped parsley*

1. In a Dutch oven or covered saucepan, combine the white navy beans with the water, bring to a boil, turn down to a simmer, cover, and cook for 1 hour.

2. In a sauté pan, heat the olive oil and sauté the chopped onions, celery, and carrots until they begin to color. Add to the bean pot along with the chopped garlic, tomato paste, lemon juice, sugar, and cayenne. Season to taste with salt.

3. Continue simmering the covered beans for another hour, until very tender.

4. Just before serving, stir in the chopped parsley. Serve hot or at room temperature.

. . . .

Notes and Variations

Try this recipe with the addition of ½ teaspoon allspice. Any haricot can be used here.
The lemon juice adds a nice bite to the beans, while the tomato paste and sugar add a subtle
sweetness. Add more garlic if you wish and more cayenne if you want it spicy hot.

. . . .

Lighter Version

Omit the olive oil, sugar, and salt.
Exchange the regular tomato paste for
low-sodium tomato paste. Add 2 more
cloves garlic and another ½ teaspoon
cayenne pepper.

NUTRITIONAL ANALYSIS

	Regular		Lighter Version	
Calories:	464		305	
Protein:	18	g	18	g
Carbohydrates:	59	g	59	g
Dietary Fiber:	17	g	17	g
Fat:	19.5	g	1.5	g
Cholesterol:	0	mg	0	mg
Sodium:	885	mg	55	mg

Percent of Calories

Protein:	15 %	22 %
Carbohydrates:	49 %	74 %
Fat:	36 %	4 %

TURKISH
WHITE HARICOT SALAD

Serves 8 as a salad

1   *pound dried white haricot beans*

8   *cups water, or more if necessary*

2   *teaspoons salt*

½   *teaspoon white pepper*

2   *medium onions, thinly sliced*

2   *tablespoons white vinegar*

¼   *cup fresh lemon juice*

½   *cup light-flavored (yellow) olive oil*

1   *tablespoon chopped fresh mint*

2   *tablespoons chopped fresh dill*

¼   *cup chopped fresh parsley*

1   *medium sweet green bell pepper, seeded and thinly sliced*

3   *hard-boiled eggs, quartered*

1. Soak the beans overnight or quick-soak. Drain the beans and combine with the water in a pot. Bring to a simmer, cover, and cook for 1 ½ hours. Add the salt and pepper and cook for another 30 minutes, until tender. Drain the beans and transfer to a salad bowl.

2. While the beans are still hot, add the sliced onions. Fold in the vinegar, lemon juice, olive oil, mint, dill, and parsley. Let cool to room temperature.

3. Cover and refrigerate the beans for at least 2 hours.

4. Before serving, garnish the bean salad with the green pepper and eggs.

. . . .

Notes and Variations

Don't overcook the beans. They should be whole, no cracked skins, with a little bite left. Quarter the eggs just before serving so they will not have time to discolor. They can be sliced into rounds rather than quarters or they can be diced. The beans are cooled at room temperature before refrigerating because they absorb more of the added flavors at room temperature.

. . . .

Lighter Version

Omit the salt and olive oil. Increase the measures of white vinegar, mint, and dill by 1 tablespoon each.

NUTRITIONAL ANALYSIS

	Regular		Lighter Version	
Calories:	367		254	
Protein:	15	g	15	g
Carbohydrates:	42.5	g	44	g
Dietary Fiber:	11.5	g	11.3	g
Fat:	16.3	g	2.8	g
Cholesterol:	79.5	mg	79	mg
Sodium:	575	mg	44	mg

Percent of Calories

Protein:	16 %	23 %
Carbohydrates:	45 %	68 %
Fat:	39 %	10 %

WHITE BEAN SALAD   *Serves 8 as a salad or an appetizer*

1   *pound white haricot beans, soaked overnight*
1   *cup water*
½   *cup fruity olive oil*
¼   *cup red wine vinegar*
1   *large onion, chopped*
2   *cloves garlic, minced*
2   *tablespoons chopped parsley*
4   *hard-boiled eggs, chopped*
2   *teaspoons salt or to taste*
1   *teaspoon white pepper or to taste*

1. In a bean pot, combine the soaked white haricot beans and water and bring to a boil. Turn down to a simmer and cook for 1½ hours, until the beans are tender but still slightly firm to the bite. Do not cook them soft. Drain the beans, transfer to a bowl, and chill in the refrigerator.

2. When the beans are chilled, add the olive oil, red wine vinegar, chopped onion, minced garlic, chopped parsley, chopped eggs, and season with salt and pepper.

3. Toss and serve.

Notes and Variations

Black pepper or ½ teaspoon cayenne pepper can be used in place of the white pepper. You can give this simple bean salad a new twist with the simple addition of capers, olives, or a diced tomato. A red onion or Vidalia onion would sweeten the taste of the completed salad and lessen the raw onion taste. Add a chopped fresh herb for more flavor levels — try 2 tablespoons chopped fresh basil or cilantro or 1 tablespoon chopped oregano.

Lighter Version

Omit the olive oil and salt. Replace the 4 hard-boiled eggs with 8 hard-boiled egg whites. Increase the vinegar by 2 tablespoons, the garlic by 2 cloves, and the parsley by 2 tablespoons.

NUTRITIONAL ANALYSIS

	Regular		Lighter Version	
Calories:	360		223	
Protein:	15.5	g	16	g
Carbohydrates:	39	g	39	g
Dietary Fiber:	11	g	11	g
Fat:	17	g	<1	g
Cholesterol:	106	mg	0	mg
Sodium:	572	mg	115	mg

Percent of Calories

Protein:	17%	28%
Carbohydrates:	42%	69%
Fat:	41%	3%

WHITE BEAN PIE

Makes one 9-inch pie   Serves 6

2 cups soft-cooked white beans, cooled and drained
  (no salt or seasoning in cooking water)
2 large eggs
1 cup white granulated sugar
½ cup heavy cream
2 teaspoons vanilla extract
¼ teaspoon ground ginger
⅛ teaspoon grated nutmeg
⅛ teaspoon ground cinnamon
½ teaspoon salt
1 9-inch piecrust

1. Pass the beans through a tamis or china cap to express the meat from the shells of the beans. Discard the shells and puree the meat or pulp. Or you can process the whole beans into a puree.

2. In a mixing bowl or in the food processor, combine the bean puree with the eggs, sugar, and heavy cream. Add the vanilla, ginger, nutmeg, cinnamon, and salt.

3. Pour the pie filling into a 9-inch piecrust on a cookie sheet and place in a preheated 350°F oven. Bake for 30 minutes, until the tip of a small knife comes out clean after inserting it into the center of the pie.

4. Remove the pie from the oven and cool on a rack. Serve.

Notes and Variations

The final texture of the pie is lighter and creamier if the bean shells or skins are removed and only the flesh or pulp is used. Use brown sugar in place of the white; it is richer in flavor. Add more sugar if you desire a sweeter pie. Grate the nutmeg yourself for better flavor.

Use fresh minced or pressed ginger if you have any — 1½ teaspoons. Another nice addition is a tablespoon of dark rum or bourbon. One-half cup chopped pecans sautéed in 2 tablespoons butter can be added to the pie filling before baking. I prefer to place the piecrust in the heated oven and fill it using a ladle.

Lighter Version

Bean pie is fairly unusual and should be made with the richness of the ingredients I have used here. A lighter version just might not be as appealing, so I have not ventured one.

NUTRITIONAL ANALYSIS

Regular

Calories:	420	
Protein:	9	g
Carbohydrates:	60	g
Dietary Fiber:	4	g
Fat:	16	g
Cholesterol:	98	mg
Sodium:	362	mg

Percent of Calories

Protein:	9%
Carbohydrates:	57%
Fat:	35%

Other White Bean Preparations

— If you're looking for more fiber, more protein, and fewer empty calories in your diet, use pureed white beans, or just seasoned boiled beans where you would serve cooked rice or mashed potatoes.

— Serve with tomato sauce and grated Parmesan cheese.

— Serve boiled and marinated in brine or a vinaigrette as a snack instead of peanuts or chips.

— Keep some cooked in the refrigerator to add to any dish such as salads, baked vegetables, soups, purees, or casseroles.

Pinto Beans

Pony Bean, Appaloosa Bean, Speckled Bean

Phaseolus vulgaris

ORIGIN: CENTRAL AMERICA

Pinto beans are members of the same family as red bean, black bean, white bean, and green bean and can be used in any recipe that uses the other beans.

To American cooks, they have been traditionally used in Mexican, Southwest, and Tex-Mex dishes.

BOILED BEANS

Serves 6

1 *pound pinto beans, soaked*

8 *cups water*

2 *tablespoons lard (traditional), bacon drippings, or olive oil*

1 *medium yellow onion, chopped*

2 *garlic cloves, chopped*

1 *teaspoon cumin*

1 *teaspoon dried epazote (optional), or oregano*

2 *teaspoons salt*

1 *dried chili pepper, minced, or to taste*

. . . .

1. Boil the beans in the water for 1 hour, until they begin to become tender.

2. Heat the drippings or lard in a sauté pan and sauté the chopped onion and garlic. Add to the beans along with the remaining ingredients.

3. Simmer for another ½ hour, until the beans are at your desired tenderness.

. . . .

Notes and Variations

Epazote is difficult to find; usually I can find it in herb/pepper catalogs. It once was the principal herb used for flavoring beans in the Americas. I generally use oregano in its place.

. . . .

Lighter Version

Omit the lard or other oil and the salt.
Increase the epazote or oregano by
1 teaspoon and the garlic by 2 cloves.
Add 2 teaspoons vinegar.

NUTRITIONAL ANALYSIS

	Regular		Lighter Version	
Calories:	292		256	
Protein:	15	g	15	g
Carbohydrates:	48	g	48	g
Dietary Fiber:	15.5	g	15.5	g
Fat:	5.3	g	1	g
Cholesterol:	4	mg	0	mg
Sodium:	715	mg	5	mg

Percent of Calories

Protein:	20%	20%
Carbohydrates:	64%	64%
Fat:	16%	16%

PINTO BEAN PUREE

Simply drain the liquids from the Boiled Beans in the previous recipe
and mash the beans together into a mass. Heat only long enough to dissipate
excess liquid. Season as desired.

REFRIED BEANS

Serves 6

    1 pound dried pinto beans, cooked soft

    3 tablespoons lard or bacon drippings (traditional) or olive oil

    1 large yellow onion, minced

    2 cloves garlic, minced

    1 teaspoon ground cumin

    2 teaspoons salt

1. Heat the lard or drippings and sauté the onion and garlic until lightly browned.

2. Add the beans and fry, and stir until the beans are mashed into a manageable mash.

3. Season with cumin and salt.

Notes and Variations

Refried beans are good alone or garnished with a little Mexican fresh cheese or Parmesan. Any dried bean can be used in place of the pinto; black and red beans are the most popular replacements.

Lighter Version

Omit the lard or other oil and the salt. Increase the garlic by 1 clove and the cumin by ½ teaspoon. Add 2 teaspoons vinegar.

NUTRITIONAL ANALYSIS

	Regular		Lighter Version	
Calories:	313		257	
Protein:	15	g	15	g
Carbohydrates:	49	g	49	g
Dietary Fiber:	16	g	16	g
Fat:	12	g	1	g
Cholesterol:	10	mg	0	mg
Sodium:	372	mg	5	mg

Percent of Calories

Protein:	19 %	23 %
Carbohydrates:	60 %	74 %
Fat:	21 %	4 %

PINTO BEAN CHILI

Serves 6 as an entree

1   pound dried pinto beans, soaked
8   cups water
4   bay leaves
¼   cup lard (traditional), bacon drippings, or olive oil
3   large onions, chopped
2   large bell peppers, chopped
2   large celery ribs, chopped
2   large tomatoes, diced
6   cloves garlic, chopped
2   jalapeños, seeded and minced
2   tablespoons chili powder
1   tablespoon dried cumin or to taste
2   teaspoons oregano
2   teaspoons salt
1   teaspoon black pepper
½   cup chopped cilantro

1. In a bean pot, simmer the pinto beans in the water with the bay leaves for about 1 hour, until tender. Hold aside in the cooking liquor.

2. In a large sauté pan, heat the olive oil and sauté the chopped onions, bell peppers, and celery until limp.

3. Add the tomatoes, garlic, jalapeños, chili powder, cumin, and oregano.

4. Add the cooked pintos in their liquor to the pan and season with salt and black pepper. Add more jalapeño or other pepper of your choice if desired.

5. Cover and simmer for 1 hour, until the beans are very tender. Add more water during the cooking if you want a looser pinto bean chili. Uncover and simmer off the excess liquid if you want a thicker chili. Remove the bay leaves.

6. A few minutes before serving, fold in the fresh cilantro and adjust the seasonings and peppers if desired.

Notes and Variations

Any peppers of your preference can be used in place of the jalapeño. Jalapeño remains the easiest to find fresh in the grocery. Add a little fresh lime juice at the end of cooking. Any dried bean will work in place of the pinto. Of course, any meats can be used here. Just cube or grind and fry the meat in the fat before you add the onions and other vegetables. I would use about half the volume of meat to beans. Beef, pork, and poultry can be used. The best chili to my personal taste is made with pork. With meat added the chili will serve 8 to 10.

Lighter Version

Omit the lard or other oil and the salt.
Add 1 tablespoon cider vinegar.

NUTRITIONAL ANALYSIS

	Regular		Lighter Version	
Calories:	401		325	
Protein:	17	g	17	g
Carbohydrates:	62	g	62	g
Dietary Fiber:	19	g	19	g
Fat:	11	g	2	g
Cholesterol:	8.1	mg	0	mg
Sodium:	762	mg	52	mg

Percent of Calories

Protein:	17 %	21 %
Carbohydrates:	60 %	74 %
Fat:	23 %	6 %

PINTO BEAN AND SPINACH SOUP WITH SHRIMP

Serves 8

- 1 *pound pinto beans, soaked*
- 12 *cups water*
- 1 *pound raw shrimp, with heads and shells on*
- 1 *teaspoon anise seeds*
- 3 *tablespoons olive oil*
- 1 *large onion, chopped*
- 2 *ribs celery, chopped*
- 6 *cloves garlic, chopped*
- 6 *bay leaves*
- 1 *teaspoon thyme leaves*
- 2 *teaspoons salt*
- 1 *teaspoon black pepper*
- ½ *teaspoon cayenne pepper*
- 1 *bag spinach, rinsed and stemmed*
- 2 *green onions, chopped*
- ¼ *cup chopped parsley*

1. Simmer the pinto beans in 8 cups of the water until tender, about 1 hour.

2. Remove the heads, peel, and devein the raw shrimp. Salt lightly, cover, and refrigerate. Put the heads and shells in a pot with 4 cups water and the anise seeds. Bring to a boil and cook for about 7 minutes to make a shrimp stock. Drain the shrimp stock in a colander, mashing the heads and shells to press out any remaining fat or liquid. Discard the heads and shells and add the shrimp stock to the bean pot.

3. In a sauté pan, heat the olive oil and sauté the chopped onion, celery, and garlic with the bay leaves until the vegetables brown somewhat. Add to the bean pot.

4. Add the thyme, salt, black pepper, and cayenne. Simmer for 5 minutes.

5. Add the spinach, cover the pot, and simmer for 10 minutes, until the spinach is very tender. Remove the bay leaves.

6. Add the reserved shrimp and cook for about 2 minutes.

7. Adjust the seasonings if desired, add the chopped green onions, and parsley and serve in soup bowls.

. . . .

Notes and Variations

Any haricot beans can be used here: red, white, or black. The anise seeds can be substituted with tarragon or omitted completely. I rinse the spinach but don't discard any of the product at all. I like the stems and the varying consistency it gives the final dish. Chop it if you want smaller pieces in the soup. I like the whole leaves to curl up on my spoon. I use the smallest (and least expensive) shrimp. Chop the shrimp if you want better distribution in the soup.

. . . .

Lighter Version

Omit the olive oil and salt. Increase the garlic by 3 cloves and thyme by 1 teaspoon.

NUTRITIONAL ANALYSIS

	Regular		Lighter Version	
Calories:	316		273	
Protein:	24.5	g	24.5	g
Carbohydrates:	40.5	g	41	g
Dietary Fiber:	14	g	14	g
Fat:	7	g	2	g
Cholesterol:	86	mg	86	mg
Sodium:	675	mg	143	mg

Percent of Calories

Protein:	30%	35%
Carbohydrates:	50%	58%
Fat:	20%	7%

Cranberry Beans

Roman Bean

Phaseolus vulgaris
ORIGIN: CENTRAL AMERICA

In most cases, the cranberry bean seems to be the name used for the red bean in the American Northeast as well as Central Europe. In Italy they are called Roman beans, but "Roman" is not meant to imply that the early Romans had them. They are Central American and did not come to Italy until the early sixteenth century. Cranberry beans can be used in any recipe that calls for dried beans.

BOILED CRANBERRY BEANS

Serves 6

1 *pound beans, soaked*
8 *cups water*
Salt to taste
Freshly ground black pepper to taste

. . . .

1. Simmer the beans in the water for 1½ hours, or long enough to achieve the tenderness desired for any specific recipe.

2. Season to taste with salt and pepper.

. . . .

Notes and Variations

Seasoning meats and vegetables should be added to the beans to flavor as you desire. The analysis is given without any salt or other ingredients.

NUTRITIONAL ANALYSIS

Calories:	239	
Protein:	16.5	g
Carbohydrates:	43	g
Dietary Fiber:	14	g
Fat:	<1	g
Cholesterol:	0	mg
Sodium:	2	mg

Percent of Calories

Protein:	27%
Carbohydrates:	70%
Fat:	3%

ROMAN BEAN AND TOMATO SALAD

Serves 6 as an entree

- 1 pound dried Roman beans, soaked, boiled, drained, and chilled
- 1½ pounds plum tomatoes, diced
- 6 green onions, chopped
- ¾ cup fruity green olive oil
- ⅓ cup red wine vinegar
- 4 tablespoons capers
- 2 tablespoons chopped fresh basil leaves
- 1½ tablespoons chopped fresh oregano leaves
- 1 tablespoon chopped fresh rosemary leaves
- 2 cloves garlic, pressed
- 2 teaspoons salt or to taste
- 1 teaspoon white pepper

1. Place the cooked, chilled beans in a salad bowl.
2. Add the tomatoes and green onions and toss with the beans.
3. Add all the remaining ingredients and toss thoroughly.
4. Adjust the seasonings as desired.

Notes and Variations

The beans should be boiled only to a tender, not soft, stage. This same recipe works well with fava beans and chickpeas. Add more tomatoes, if you prefer.

Lighter Version

Omit the olive oil and salt. Increase the vinegar from ⅓ to ½ cup and the garlic from 2 to 4 cloves.

NUTRITIONAL ANALYSIS

	Regular	Lighter Version
Calories:	523	288
Protein:	18.4 g	18.4 g
Carbohydrates:	53 g	55 g
Dietary Fiber:	16.5 g	16.5 g
Fat:	28.3 g	1.3 g
Cholesterol:	0 mg	0 mg
Sodium:	937 mg	226 mg

Percent of Calories

Protein:	14 %	24 %
Carbohydrates:	40 %	72 %
Fat:	47 %	4 %

ROMAN BEANS AND PASTA WITH OIL AND GARLIC

Serves 6 as an entree

1 *pound dried Roman beans, boiled, drained and hot*
1 *pound dried small pasta, boiled, drained, and hot*
1 *cup yellow olive oil*
2 *whole heads garlic, cloves peeled and lightly crushed*
2 *tablespoons dried rosemary*
2 *tablespoons dried oregano*
2 *teaspoons salt*
2 *teaspoons freshly ground black pepper*
½ *cup dry vermouth*

1. Cook the beans and pasta so they are ready.

2. Heat the olive oil in a large pan and add the garlic, rosemary, oregano, salt, black pepper, and vermouth. Simmer for just a minute or two.

3. Add the beans and fold around into the pan sauce until all is well coated and very hot.

4. Serve the beans with grated cheese on the side and lots of crusty bread to dip in the pan juices.

. . . .

Notes and Variations

The beans are the base of the recipe, but the sauce can be your choice: Try a marinara or a puttanesca, or any tomato sauce. And don't forget the grated cheese. This recipe can serve 8 to 10 smaller portions.

. . . .

Lighter Version

Prepare this recipe by eliminating the oil and salt. Begin by cooking the garlic dry in the pan until it begins to color, then add the vermouth and 1 cup chicken, beef, or shellfish stock made without salt, and the remaining ingredients.

NUTRITIONAL ANALYSIS

	Regular		Lighter Version	
Calories:	853		538	
Protein:	26	g	26.7	g
Carbohydrates:	99	g	99	g
Dietary Fiber:	17.5	g	17.5	g
Fat:	38	g	2	g
Cholesterol:	0	mg	0	mg
Sodium:	720	mg	21	mg

Percent of Calories

Protein:	12 %	20 %
Carbohydrates:	46 %	73 %
Fat:	40 %	4 %

CRANBERRY BEAN MINESTRONE   *Serves 8*

1 *pound fresh cranberry beans*
½ *cup light-flavored olive oil*
1 *large onion, chopped*
1 *medium carrot, chopped*
1 *rib celery, stringed and diced*
2 *garlic cloves, minced or pressed*
1 *small sweet green bell pepper, seeded and chopped*
2 *tablespoons chopped parsley*
1 *teaspoon anise seeds*
2 *teaspoons crushed dried basil leaves, chopped*
1 *teaspoon dried oregano*
1 *teaspoon dried marjoram*
3 *medium tomatoes, skinned, seeded, and chopped*
1½ *quarts beef stock*
½ *cup red wine*
½ *cup broken vermicelli*
2 *cups chopped fresh spinach*
2 *teaspoons salt*
1 *teaspoon freshly ground black pepper or to taste*
½ *cup grated Parmesan cheese*

1. Shell the cranberry beans and discard the pods.

2. Heat the olive oil in a soup pot or large saucepan and add the chopped onion. Cook until translucent.

3. Add the shelled cranberry beans, carrot, celery, garlic, bell pepper, parsley, anise, basil, oregano, marjoram, chopped tomatoes, and the beef stock. Bring to a boil, cover, reduce to a gentle simmer, and cook for about 30 minutes, until the beans are tender.

4. Uncover the pot, add the red wine and vermicelli and continue simmering until the pasta is tender.

5. Add the chopped spinach and cook for 2 minutes more. Season to taste with salt and freshly ground black pepper.

6. Serve the soup with 1 tablespoon grated Parmesan cheese sprinkled over each serving.

. . . .

Notes and Variations

If you have fresh herbs — basil, oregano, marjoram — use them in place of the dried: three times the amount of dried. Most of this country is not as familiar with the cranberry bean as the other haricot beans. This minestrone can be made with any haricot bean — red, black, white, or pinto. Simply presoak the dried beans and cook until tender. Proceed as for the fresh cranberry beans. Skin the tomatoes by dropping them into boiling water for about 45 seconds, remove the tomatoes from the water, and peel away the loose skin. The vermicelli pasta can be replaced with angel hair or any shaped small pasta of your preference. This recipe makes a very rich minestrone. If you find it too dense for your taste, thin it with more stock or water.

. . . .

Lighter Version

Omit the olive oil and salt. Cook the onion dry in the pan by stirring constantly over the heat until it begins to color. Replace the beef stock with low-sodium, nonfat beef stock and the Parmesan cheese with nonfat Parmesan cheese. Increase the measures of basil, oregano, and marjoram by 1 teaspoon each.

NUTRITIONAL ANALYSIS

	Regular		Lighter Version	
Calories:	322		198	
Protein:	12.5	g	15	g
Carbohydrates:	31	g	33	g
Dietary Fiber:	8	g	8	g
Fat:	16.5	g	<1	g
Cholesterol:	5	mg	5	mg
Sodium:	1543	mg	656	mg

Percent of Calories		
Protein:	15%	29%
Carbohydrates:	38%	63%
Fat:	44%	4%

HUNGARIAN CRANBERRY BEAN SOUP

Serves 10

1 pig's foot, split

2 smoked ham hocks

1 pound dried cranberry beans, soaked overnight

2½ quarts water

2 tablespoons lard (traditional) or oil

2 medium onions, chopped

2 ribs celery, chopped

2 tablespoons flour

4 cloves garlic, chopped

2 tablespoons chopped parsley

1 tablespoon hot Hungarian paprika

2 cups hot water

½ pound smoked pork sausage, cut into ½-inch thick rounds

2 teaspoons salt or to taste

1 teaspoon freshly ground black pepper or to taste

½ cup sour cream

. . . .

1. In a soup pot or large saucepan, combine the split pig's foot, smoked ham hocks, dried cranberry beans, and water. Bring to a boil, cover, and turn down to a gentle simmer. Cook for 1 hour, until the meat on the pig's foot and ham hocks is very tender.

2. Carefully lift the split pig's foot and the ham hocks out of the beans to a plate or cutting board. Remove the meat from the bones. Dice the meat and return it to the pot. Discard the bones.

3. In a sauté pan, heat the lard and sauté the chopped onions and celery until translucent. Carefully blend in the flour and cook together until this roux achieves a rich brown color. Stir in the garlic, parsley, and paprika. Whisk in the 2 cups hot water and add this mixture to the bean pot.

4. Add the pork sausage, season to taste with salt and freshly ground black pepper, and simmer gently for ½ hour more, until the cranberry beans are very tender.

5. Just before serving, remove the soup from the heat and stir in the sour cream.

. . . .

Notes and Variations

The pig's foot and the smoked ham hocks add richness in flavor and texture to the soup broth. They are not absolutely necessary and can be done without, provided you increase the sausage measure from ½ to 1 pound. The lard can be replaced with butter or any preferred oil. The cranberry beans can be replaced with any haricot bean.

. . . .

Lighter Version

Omit the pig's foot, ham hocks, lard, and salt. Cook the seasoning vegetables and flour together in a nonstick pan until the mixture begins to color. Stir constantly to avoid burning. Replace the ½ pound smoked pork sausage with ½ pound low-fat turkey sausage, preferably smoked. Add a teaspoon of liquid smoke if you have it. This will replace the smoke flavor from the smoked ham hocks. Replace the sour cream with nonfat sour cream. Add 2 packets of plain gelatin.

NUTRITIONAL ANALYSIS

	Regular		Lighter Version	
Calories:	407		253	
Protein:	24.5	g	17.5	g
Carbohydrates:	38.5	g	40.5	g
Dietary Fiber:	12	g	12	g
Fat:	17.5	g	3	g
Cholesterol:	45	mg	14	mg
Sodium:	848	mg	223	mg

Percent of Calories

Protein:	24 %	27 %
Carbohydrates:	38 %	63 %
Fat:	39 %	10 %

Lima Beans

Butter Bean, Sugar Bean, Habas, Burma Bean, Guffin Bean, Hibbert Bean, Java Bean, Sieva Bean, Rangoon Bean, Duffin, Madagascar Bean, Paiga, Paigya, Prolific Bean, Civet Bean, Cachas, Huevo de Piche, Pallars, Zaragosa

Phaseolus lunatus or Phaseolus limensis (synonym)
ORIGIN: CENTRAL AMERICA

Small bean varieties were domesticated in MesoAmerica; large bean varieties were domesticated in South America.

The lima bean can vary from a flattened seed to a more plumped, full seed. Colors vary from white, cream, green, red, purple, brown, or black. Some are mottled versions of these colors.

Lima beans are grown for use as green shell beans or as dried beans or pulse. The immature pods and leaves are used by some as vegetables.

Limas are more available fresh/frozen than most dried beans. Use 3 pounds fresh/frozen for each pound dried in these recipes. Frozen limas require only about 15 minutes of boiling, while dried require an hour or more.

BOILED LIMA BEANS

Serves 6 as a side

1 *pound dried lima beans, soaked*
8 *cups water*
Salt to taste
Freshly ground black pepper to taste

. . . .

1. Simmer the limas in the water for about 1 hour.

2. Season to taste with salt and pepper.

. . . .

Notes and Variations

Since limas come dried in a variety of sizes, the cooking time will vary. For added taste and richness add 2 to 3 tablespoons of butter and 2 tablespoons chopped parsley. Some minced green onions are also a nice addition. This analysis is given without salt added.

NUTRITIONAL ANALYSIS

Calories:	253	
Protein:	14	g
Carbohydrates:	48.5	g
Dietary Fiber:	11	g
Fat:	<1	g
Cholesterol:	0	mg
Sodium:	228	mg

Percent of Calories

Protein:	22%
Carbohydrates:	75%
Fat:	3%

BUTTER BEANS IN ROUX

Serves 6 as a side

4 *tablespoons butter*

4 *tablespoons flour*

1 *medium onion, chopped*

2 *ribs celery, chopped*

1 *pound dried small lima beans, boiled, reserve liquor*

2 *teaspoons salt or to taste*

1 *teaspoon white pepper*

2 *tablespoons chopped parsley*

. . . .

1. Heat the butter in a large pan and blend in the flour. Stir and cook into an amber roux.

2. Add the chopped onion and celery. Cook together for just 2 minutes.

3. Add about a cup of the lima liquor and whisk until smooth.

4. Add the cooked lima beans, blending well with the roux and heating well.

5. Season to taste with salt and white pepper.

6. Stir in the parsley and serve.

. . . .

Notes and Variations

Another fresh herb can replace the parsley: basil, tarragon, cilantro, oregano, or mint. This can make a simple entree served over rice.

· ·

Lighter Version

Lighten the recipe by omitting the salt and butter. Cook the flour dry in a pan, stirring constantly until it begins to color. Then whisk in the liquid, add the chopped vegetables, and continue with the recipe.

NUTRITIONAL ANALYSIS

	Regular		Lighter Version	
Calories:	350		283	
Protein:	16.5	g	16.5	g
Carbohydrates:	54	g	54	g
Dietary Fiber:	15	g	15	g
Fat:	8.5	g	<1	g
Cholesterol:	20.7	mg	0	mg
Sodium:	811	mg	23	mg

Percent of Calories

Protein:	19 %		23 %	
Carbohydrates:	60 %		75 %	
Fat:	21 %		3 %	

BABY GREEN LIMA BEANS WITH HAM

Serves 8 as a side

1   *pound dried baby green lima beans, soaked*
8   *cups water*
½   *pound ham*
1   *tablespoon bacon drippings or shortening*
1   *onion, chopped*
1   *clove garlic, chopped*
1   *tablespoon chopped parsley*
2   *teaspoons salt or to taste*

1. Combine the baby green lima beans, water, and seasoning meat and bring to a simmer. Cover and cook for 1 hour.

2. In a pan, heat the bacon drippings or shortening and brown the chopped onion, garlic, and parsley. Add to the beans.

3. Simmer for another 30 minutes, until the beans are tender and the liquid is thickened.

Notes and Variations

The seasoning meat can be ham, sausage, pickled pork, salt pork, or bacon. The bacon drippings can be replaced with shortening, oil, or butter. Large dried limas or fresh or frozen limas can be used here — use 3 pounds of fresh or frozen. This recipe can be served over rice as an entree.

Lighter Version

Omit the bacon drippings and salt.
Replace the ham with a low-fat ham.
Add 2 more cloves garlic and 2 more
tablespoons chopped parsley.

NUTRITIONAL ANALYSIS

	Regular		Lighter Version	
Calories:	205		111	
Protein:	15	g	10	g
Carbohydrates:	16.5	g	17.5	g
Dietary Fiber:	3	g	3	g
Fat:	10	g	1.5	g
Cholesterol:	30	mg	15	mg
Sodium:	1083	mg	347	mg

Percent of Calories

Protein:	28%	33%
Carbohydrates:	31%	57%
Fat:	41%	10%

BABY GREEN LIMA BEANS AND COLLARD GREENS

Serves 6 as an entree

1	pound dried baby green lima beans, soaked
1½	quarts chicken stock
4	tablespoons butter
1	large onion, chopped
1	small sweet green bell pepper, chopped
1	rib celery, chopped
4	large cloves garlic, chopped
4	bay leaves
½	teaspoon white pepper
¼	teaspoon cayenne pepper
1	bunch collard greens, rough chopped, approximately 2 quarts
2	teaspoons salt or to taste
¼	cup chopped parsley

1. Put the limas and stock in a saucepan and bring to a boil. Turn down to a gentle simmer, cover, and cook for 45 minutes.

2. Heat the butter in a sauté pan and sauté the chopped onion, sweet green bell pepper, celery, and garlic until the vegetables color lightly. Add to the limas along with the bay leaves, white pepper, and cayenne.

3. Add the chopped collard greens and salt and cover and continue cooking for 45 minutes more, until the beans are tender and the liquid in the pot has thickened into a sauce consistency. Stir occasionally, gently, to prevent sticking and scorching. Add water as you cook, if necessary.

4. Fold in the chopped parsley and serve in bowls.

. . . .

Notes and Variations

Dried baby green lima beans can be soaked for as little as 3 hours if desired. The chicken stock can be replaced with water. Collards in a bunch can vary in quantity. Use one complete bunch, no matter the size. Mustard greens, turnip greens, or spinach can replace the collards.

. . . .

Lighter Version

Omit the butter and salt. Replace the regular chicken stock with water. Add 2 teaspoons dried tarragon or oregano.

NUTRITIONAL ANALYSIS

	Regular		Lighter Version	
Calories:	241		137	
Protein:	13	g	8	g
Carbohydrates:	29	g	28.5	g
Dietary Fiber:	6.5	g	6.5	g
Fat:	9.7	g	<1	g
Cholesterol:	20.7	mg	0	mg
Sodium:	1585	mg	20	mg

Percent of Calories

Protein:	20%	21%
Carbohydrates:	46%	75%
Fat:	34%	4%

ISRAELI LIMA BEAN STEW

Serves 6

1   *pound dried lima beans, soaked overnight*

8   *cups water*

4   *tablespoons lard (traditional) or olive oil*

3   *pounds beef short ribs, separated*

4   *medium onions, chopped*

4   *cloves garlic, chopped*

1   *cup pearl barley, rinsed*

2   *teaspoons salt or to taste*

1   *teaspoon freshly ground black pepper or to taste*

1   *tablespoon paprika*

12 *small new potatoes, scrubbed*

1. In a saucepan or bean pot, combine the soaked lima beans with the water, place on the heat, and bring to a simmer. Cover and simmer gently for 45 minutes, until the limas are tender but not overly so.

2. Meanwhile, in a skillet, heat the lard and brown the beef short ribs on all sides. Transfer the ribs to the bean pot.

3. Add the chopped onions to the remaining lard in the skillet. Sauté until the onions just begin to color, add the chopped garlic and sauté together for 1 minute more. Transfer the sautéed onions and garlic to the bean pot.

4. Stir in the rinsed pearl barley, season with salt and freshly ground black pepper, and add the paprika and new potatoes.

5. Cover the pot and simmer very, very gently for another hour, until the pearl barley is tender. Add more water during the cooking if necessary.

Notes and Variations

Any dried bean or pea can be used in this recipe. Replace the lard with corn or peanut oil. Pork ribs can replace the beef short ribs. Use a good-quality paprika or you will get color but no flavor.

Lighter Version

Omit the lard and salt. Replace the ribs with 1½ pounds lean stew meat. Cook the beef, onions, and garlic dry in a nonstick pan, stirring constantly while cooking to prevent burning. Add an additional ½ tablespoon paprika.

NUTRITIONAL ANALYSIS

	Regular		Lighter Version	
Calories:	650		526	
Protein:	32	g	35.5	g
Carbohydrates:	68	g	68.5	g
Dietary Fiber:	12	g	12	g
Fat:	29	g	13.5	g
Cholesterol:	71	mg	75	mg
Sodium:	754	mg	72	mg

Percent of Calories

Protein:	19 %	27 %
Carbohydrates:	41 %	51 %
Fat:	39 %	22 %

BABY GREEN LIMA BEAN, TOMATO, AND CHEESE CASSEROLE

Serves 6

- 1 *pound dried baby green lima beans, soaked*
- 6 *cups water*
- 1½ *teaspoons salt*
- 2 *tablespoons vegetable oil*
- 1 *medium onion, chopped*
- 2 *medium tomatoes, chopped*
- 1 *teaspoon chili powder*
- 1½ *cups shredded Cheddar cheese*

1. Gently simmer the dried baby green lima beans, covered, in the water for 1 hour, until the beans are soft and the liquid is thickened. Add 1 teaspoon salt.

2. Heat the vegetable oil in a skillet and brown the chopped onion. Add the chopped tomatoes, chili powder, and 1½ teaspoons salt. Simmer until thickened.

3. Grease a casserole dish and add 2 alternating layers each of the beans, onion-tomato mixture, and cheese.

4. Bake in a 350°F preheated oven for 30 minutes, until most of the liquid is reduced and the top is lightly browned.

. . . .

Notes and Variations

Add water, if necessary, during the cooking, remembering that you want the bean liquid to be thick when transferred to the casserole for baking. For better flavor, use bacon drippings in place of the vegetable oil. Add more chili powder if you desire. Another cheese of your preference can be substituted for the Cheddar — try Swiss.

. . . .

Lighter Version

Eliminate the salt and vegetable oil. Substitute a low-fat, low-sodium Cheddar cheese for the regular Cheddar. Cook the chopped onion and tomatoes in a dry pan, without shortening or oil, stirring almost constantly to prevent sticking. Add 1 onion and 2 teaspoons chili powder.

NUTRITIONAL ANALYSIS

	Regular		Lighter Version	
Calories:	422		173	
Protein:	23	g	14	g
Carbohydrates:	51	g	26.5	g
Dietary Fiber:	15	g	5	g
Fat:	14.5	g	3	g
Cholesterol:	30	mg	6	mg
Sodium:	734	mg	23	mg

Percent of Calories

Protein:	22%		30%	
Carbohydrates:	48%		56%	
Fat:	30%		13%	

BABY GREEN LIMA BEAN AND CORNISH HEN STEW

Serves 8

1   *pound dried baby lima beans, soaked or quick-soaked*
6   *cups water or stock*
4   *small Cornish hens, halved*
3   *tablespoons peanut oil*
⅓   *cup soy sauce*
8   *cloves garlic, chopped*
4   *medium carrots, sliced into ¼-inch-thick rounds*
6   *green onions, chopped*
1   *teaspoon salt or to taste*
1   *teaspoon freshly ground black pepper or to taste*
2   *tablespoons chopped parsley*

1. Quick-soak the lima beans and change the water, using 6 cups fresh water. Bring the water to a boil and simmer for ½ hour.

2. Halve the Cornish hens and sauté in a skillet with the peanut oil until nicely colored. Remove and discard the neck and rib bones. Add the halved hens to the lima beans.

3. Add the soy sauce, garlic, carrots, and onions. Season with salt and pepper to taste.

4. Bring to a simmer, cover, and cook for another ½ hour, until the stew liquid thickens from the cooked limas.

5. Stir in the chopped parsley and serve.

. . . .

Notes and Variations

Chicken or turkey can be used in place of the Cornish hens. Frozen lima beans or large dried lima beans will produce a good dish here. Chicken stock can replace the water for a richer stew. This dish is very good served over fluffy white rice.

. . . .

Lighter Version

Skin the Cornish hens and remove any existing fat as well as the rib and neck bones. Add the hens directly to the limas. You will not use the peanut oil. Omit the salt.

NUTRITIONAL ANALYSIS

	Regular		Lighter Version	
Calories:	337		228	
Protein:	27	g	24	g
Carbohydrates:	21.5	g	21.5	g
Dietary Fiber:	1.5	g	1.5	g
Fat:	16	g	5	g
Cholesterol:	67	mg	55	mg
Sodium:	1459	mg	1151	mg

Percent of Calories

Protein:	32%	42%
Carbohydrates:	26%	38%
Fat:	42%	20%

BABY GREEN LIMA BEANS WITH
LAMB LEG STEAKS

Serves 6 as an entree

1 pound dried baby green lima beans, soaked
8 cups beef stock
3 bay leaves
1 teaspoon whole allspice
1 teaspoon green peppercorns
3 tablespoons olive oil
1½ pounds lamb leg steaks
1 large onion, chopped
1 medium green bell pepper, chopped
4 cloves garlic, chopped
2 teaspoons balsamic vinegar
2 teaspoons salt or to taste
1 cup chopped green onions

1. Rinse the limas and place in a pot with the beef stock, bay leaves, allspice, and green peppercorns. Bring to a boil, turn down to a gentle simmer, cover, and cook for 1 hour. Remove the bay leaves.

2. Add the olive oil to a skillet and sauté the lamb steaks until nicely browned on both sides. Remove the lamb and hold aside.

3. To the skillet, add the chopped onion and green bell pepper and sauté until lightly browned. Add the garlic, continue cooking for 1 minute more, and remove from the heat. Hold aside.

4. When the baby green limas have simmered for 1 hour and are beginning to become tender, add the lamb steaks and the sautéed seasoning vegetables to the pot. Add the balsamic vinegar and season with salt. Simmer for another ½ hour, until the beans are very tender and the pot liquid is thickened from the cooked beans.

5. Just before serving, fold in the chopped green onions.

Notes and Variations

The beef stock can be replaced with water. The lamb steaks can be replaced by any lamb cut. Ham, pork, or rabbit makes a good substitution for the lamb. Shrimp, too, makes a great seafood variation; add 1 ½ pounds peeled, deveined raw shrimp about 5 minutes before serving and cook long enough for the shrimp to become opaque but not tough or mealy.

If you have the heads and shells from the shrimp, simmer with 8 cups water to make a stock. Use this shrimp stock in place of the beef stock. Serve over cooked white or brown rice.

Lighter Version

Omit the olive oil and salt. Replace the beef stock with nonfat, low-sodium beef broth. Replace the 1 ½ pounds lamb steaks with ¾ pound lean lamb loin. Cook the lamb dry in a nonstick pan as well as the seasoning vegetables.

Or you can add the seasoning vegetables directly to the limas 45 minutes into the simmering. Add another teaspoon green peppercorns and another teaspoon balsamic vinegar.

NUTRITIONAL ANALYSIS

	Regular		Lighter Version	
Calories:	521		384	
Protein:	36	g	33.5	g
Carbohydrates:	52.5	g	52.5	g
Dietary Fiber:	15.5	g	15.5	g
Fat:	19	g	5	g
Cholesterol:	59	mg	36.5	mg
Sodium:	1808	mg	133	mg

Percent of Calories

Protein:	28%	34%
Carbohydrates:	40%	54%
Fat:	32%	11%

Adjuki Beans

Adanka Bean, Aduki, Adsuki, Asuki,
Azuki Bean, Chi Dow, Feijao, Field Pea,
Haricot Adjuki, Hong Xiao Dou,
Red Oriental, Tiensin Red, Adzukibohne,
Judea Adzuki, Frijol Adjuki

Vigna angularis
ORIGIN: CENTRAL CHINA

The adjuki is a small oval bean, dark red, reddish brown, or yellowish brown with a white ridge along one side. The dried bean is 5 millimeters in diameter.

The adjuki has a lighter flavor than most beans, lending it to uses not usually related to beans in the West. Most adjuki beans are used for sweet sauces, confections, pastry fillings, and even ice cream. They are also made into flour and used for sprouts. Adjuki is also roasted and used as a coffee substitute.

ADJUKI "AN"

1 *pound dried adjuki beans, soaked*
8 *cups water*
1 *pound sugar*

. . . .

1. Simmer the adjuki beans in the water until very soft, even until the skins begin to split, about 1½ hours. Drain and cool.

2. For the best paste it is necessary to eliminate as much of the seed coat as possible, retaining only the soft meat of the bean. To do this the beans are passed through a tamis or a sifting device made with a screen. The beans are mashed into the screen and the pulp passes through, leaving the tougher skin mash behind on the screen. Discard the skin mash.

3. Combine the adjuki bean pulp with the sugar and work them together until the sugar has dissolved. This measure of sugar can vary, depending on the use of the resulting product, now called "An."

. . . .

Notes and Variations

This recipe is the most common use of adjuki beans in East Asia. We should think of it as we would any sort of pastry filling: as a filling for doughnuts, as a filling between cake layers, rolled in crystallized sugar as a confection. The paste can be flavored as you wish with extracts or plum wine. It is also sometimes blended with other pastes made from chestnuts or almonds. This is sometimes pressed into decorative molds and served as tea cakes. Use this paste as a spread in the same way as you might use apple butter or peanut butter. This recipe is not sweet red bean paste, which requires a little more cooking and additional ingredients. It is important to know that in East Asian cooking, the term "red bean" applies to the adjuki bean, not the red bean of the Americas.

NUTRITIONAL ANALYSIS

This analysis is for a 1-ounce serving:

Calories:	36	
Protein:	1	g
Carbohydrates:	8	g
Dietary Fiber:	1	g
Fat:	0	g
Cholesterol:	0	mg
Sodium:	0.5	mg

Percent of Calories

Protein:	12%
Carbohydrates:	87%
Fat:	2%

CHINESE MERINGUE AND BEAN PASTE "AN" DESSERT

Serves 6 4 pieces each

Oil for frying
8 *ounces red bean paste*
6 *egg whites*
2 *tablespoons cornstarch*
½ *cup confectioners' sugar*

1. Heat the oil to 300°F.

2. Divide the bean paste into 24 pieces and roll into balls.

3. Whip the egg whites to soft peak stage and whip in the cornstarch.

4. Dip the bean balls into the egg whites and drop into the hot oil. Fry for about 2 minutes and transfer to a platter to drain. Do not overcrowd the oil or it will lower the temperature too much; work in batches.

5. When all the bean balls are cooked, transfer to plates, four per serving, and dust with confectioners' sugar.

6. Serve immediately! The egg meringue will continue to shrink as they cool.

Notes and Variations

The paste can be cut into squares and the top, bottom, and sides can be covered with storebought pound cake. Dust with powdered sugar and serve. Or roll the paste into small balls, then roll the balls in chopped nuts and sugar — much easier. It's surprising that even though so much Asian cuisine is available to Americans, dishes made from adjuki beans, especially sweets, are hard to find.

NUTRITIONAL ANALYSIS

Calories:	185	
Protein:	4.5	g
Carbohydrates:	22	g
Dietary Fiber:	1.5	g
Fat:	9	g
Cholesterol:	0	mg
Sodium:	50	mg

Percent of Calories

Protein:	10 %
Carbohydrates:	46 %
Fat:	44 %

Sweet Red Bean Paste

Makes 1 ½ to 2 quarts

- 1 *pound dried red adjuki beans, soaked*
- 8 *cups water*
- 2 *cups sugar*
- 4 *cups water*
- 2 *cups peanut oil*
- 2 *tablespoons cornstarch*
- 3 *tablespoons water*
- ½ *teaspoon salt*

1. Simmer the beans in the water for 1 ½ to 2 hours, until very soft. Drain and cool.

2. Pass the beans through a tamis or strainer to get the interior pulp but not the tougher skins. Discard the skin mash.

3. Combine the bean paste, water, and sugar in a saucepan and simmer for 15 minutes.

4. Work in 1 cup peanut oil and simmer gently for about 20 minutes. Stir on occasion to keep the oil from separating.

5. Stir in the remaining 1 cup peanut oil and simmer for another 20 to 30 minutes, stirring two to three times.

6. Combine the cornstarch with the water and quickly work it into the bean paste. Add the salt. Simmer for 7 to 10 minutes until the paste thickens and comes away from the sides of the saucepan.

7. Transfer the red bean paste to a jar, cover, and refrigerate for use as needed. The sauce will keep well for 3 weeks in the refrigerator and freezes well.

Notes and Variations

Sweet red bean paste is used in a myriad of Asian recipes to add depth, sweetness, texture, and color. I use it as I might soy sauce or teriyaki sauce to any other sauce or dish. The difference between a sweet red bean "An" is that it is used for pastry and dessert filling and the sweet red bean paste is used for sauces.

NUTRITIONAL ANALYSIS

per 1 tablespoon

Calories:	52	
Protein:	1	g
Carbohydrates:	5	g
Dietary Fiber:	.5	g
Fat:	3.5	g
Sodium:	8	mg

Percent of Calories

Protein:	5%
Carbohydrates:	38%
Fat:	57%

DUCK SAUCE

Makes 2 1/4 cups

¼ *cup sesame oil*
1 *cup sweet red bean paste*
1 *cup sugar*
1 *cup water*
1 *teaspoon salt*

. . . .

1. Heat the sesame oil in a saucepan.

2. Add the sweet red bean paste, sugar, water, and salt. Simmer for
    4 minutes, until the sauce thickens.

3. Transfer to a capped jar and refrigerate.

. . . .

Notes and Variations

Duck sauce is the traditional sauce served
with Peking Duck, thus the name. It is also
served with any other fried poultry dish as
well as roast pork. It can be used anywhere
a sweet entree sauce is desired.

NUTRITIONAL ANALYSIS

per 1-ounce serving

Calories:	81	
Protein:	.5	g
Carbohydrates:	13	g
Dietary Fiber:	.5	g
Fat:	3.5	g
Cholesterol:	0	mg
Sodium:	107	mg

Percent of Calories

Protein:	2%
Carbohydrates:	60%
Fat:	37%

HACKED CHICKEN
WITH SWEET RED BEAN PASTE   *Serves 4*

  1 3-pound chicken

  4 cups peanut oil for frying

  6 eggs, well beaten

  2 cups cornflour or cornstarch

½ cup sweet red bean paste

  1 tablespoon soy sauce or more to taste

  8 green onions, cut diagonally into 1-inch lengths

1. Cut the chicken up as for frying and then hack the pieces through the meat and bones with a cleaver or heavy knife into smaller pieces.

2. Heat the peanut oil in a frying pan or wok until it begins to smoke.

3. Dip the chicken pieces in the beaten eggs and dredge in the cornflour, or cornstarch, until completely coated.

4. Carefully place the chicken pieces in the hot oil and cook, in batches if necessary, for about 4 minutes, until each piece is done. Remove the chicken and drain.

5. Pour off all but about ½ cup oil, add the red bean paste, soy sauce, and green onions.

6. Return the chicken pieces to the pan and heat and turn the pieces until all are well coated and the green onions are cooked.

. . . .

Notes and Variations

This recipe can be made with pork, duck, shrimp, and even fish or soft-shell crab.

. . . .

Lighter Version

You can make this recipe with roasted chicken, no skin, no oil, eggs, or corn-starch. The analysis follows.

NUTRITIONAL ANALYSIS

	Regular		Lighter Version	
Calories:	615		233	
Protein:	38	g	36	g
Carbohydrates:	52	g	12	g
Dietary Fiber:	3.5	g	3	g
Fat:	27	g	4	g
Cholesterol:	310	mg	90	mg
Sodium:	861	mg	556	mg

Percent of Calories

	Regular	Lighter Version
Protein:	25%	63%
Carbohydrates:	34%	21%
Fat:	40%	16%

JAPANESE RED ADJUKI BEANS AND GLUTINOUS RICE

Serves 12 as a side

1   *cup dried red adjuki beans, soaked overnight*
4   *cups glutinous rice, soaked in 8 cups water for 1 hour, drained*
5   *cups water*

. . . .

1.   Boil the soaked adjuki beans in 4 cups water for about 1 hour, until tender. Drain and reserve the cooking liquid.

2.   In a saucepan, combine the drained beans and the drained rice with 5 cups water. Cover and simmer until the rice is cooked, about 20 minutes, and all the water has dissipated or been absorbed.

3.   Transfer the mixture to a plate and spread it out with a spatula, or mold it with custard cups.

4.   Cool and serve with wasabi, tamari, or teriyaki sauce. Sprinkle with roasted sesame seeds if you like.

. . . .

Notes and Variations

The resulting dish should hold together in a mass. It should even be able to be picked up without falling apart. This dish is very common in Japan. Try other condiments with it such as pickled ginger and pickled vegetables.

NUTRITIONAL ANALYSIS

Calories:	260	
Protein:	7.5	g
Carbohydrates:	55	g
Dietary Fiber:	5	g
Fat:	.5	g
Cholesterol:	0	mg
Sodium:	11	mg

Percent of Calories

Protein:	12 %
Carbohydrates:	86 %
Fat:	2 %

ADJUKI CREOLE

Serves 6 as an entree

1   *pound dried adjuki beans, soaked*
8   *cups water*
8   *strips bacon, diced*
2   *large onions, chopped*
4   *green onions, chopped*
2   *ribs celery, chopped*
1   *large sweet green bell pepper, chopped*
6   *cloves garlic, chopped*
¼   *cup chopped parsley*
4   *bay leaves*
2   *teaspoons dried thyme leaves*
2   *teaspoons salt*
1   *teaspoon freshly ground black pepper*

1. Combine the soaked adjuki beans and water in a large saucepan or bean pot, bring to a boil, bring down to a gentle simmer, cover, and cook for 1 hour.

2. In a sauté pan, sauté the diced bacon until all the fat is rendered and the bacon crisps. Add the chopped white onions, green onions, celery, green bell pepper, and garlic. Sauté until the seasoning vegetables are lightly browned. Add to the bean pot.

3. Add the chopped parsley, bay leaves, and thyme. Simmer for 30 minutes more. Season to taste with salt and black pepper. Simmer for another 30 minutes, until the beans are very tender. Remove the bay leaves.

Notes and Variations

Serve these beans over rice if you like. In this case the beans will serve 8 fairly substantial portions or as many as 12 appetizer or side portions. Mash some of the cooked beans against the inside wall of the pot to make a thick sauce of the pot liquid. I have added this cross-cultural recipe as an example of the adjuki's ability to be used in any dried bean recipe. The result is very good, with a lighter flavor than with the traditional western red kidney bean. I have included this recipe to show that adjuki beans can be used in western bean recipes.

Lighter Version

Omit the bacon and salt. Increase the garlic measure by 2 cloves. Add 1 whole medium diced tomato.

NUTRITIONAL ANALYSIS

	Regular		Lighter Version	
Calories:	467		362	
Protein:	23	g	20	g
Carbohydrates:	70	g	71.5	g
Dietary Fiber:	4.5	g	4.5	g
Fat:	11.5	g	<1	g
Cholesterol:	14	mg	0	mg
Sodium:	921	mg	40	mg

Percent of Calories

Protein:	19%	22%
Carbohydrates:	59%	77%
Fat:	22%	1%

Fava Beans

Broad Bean, Faba Bean, Horsebean, Windsorbean, Tickbeans, Haba Beans, Veza Beans, Bakela, Boby Kurmouvje, Faveira, Ful Masri, Ful Nabed, Feve, Yeshil Bakla, Lucky Bean (New Orleans)

Vicia faba
ORIGIN: SOUTHERN EUROPE

Immature pods of the fava or broad bean are cooked as for green beans. The shelled beans, fresh or rehydrated from dry, are used in almost all of Europe and the Mediterranean areas. The beans are edible roasted and are milled into flour.

Favas can be found canned in differing stages of growth from green and small to large green broad beans. Favas are eaten as breakfast food in the Mediterranean and the Middle East, as well as China and Ethiopia.

A more popular dish in these areas is the medamis, which is stewed fava beans. Another dish is deep-fried falafel, made from seasoned fried, mashed beans.

Fava beans require longer soaking than other beans due to their tough skin. Unless the bean is fresh or small, the skin is usually removed from the soaked or cooked bean, making it a work intensive bean to use, but well worth the time. Some people prefer to leave on the skins for the slightly bitter and distinctive flavor they add to any preparation.

BOILED FAVA BEANS

Serves 6

1   *pound dried fava beans, soaked from 12 to 48 hours, depending on size*
10 *cups water, or more if necessary*

. . . .

1. Simmer the beans in the water for 3 hours, until tender. Drain and cool.

2. Use a small knife like a chestnut or paring knife, or even your fingernail to cut the bean skin at the thin side ridge and squeeze the bean out. Discard the skins.

3. The beans can now be used as any dried bean or simply marinated in a vinaigrette as appetizers.

. . . .

Notes and Variations

Fava beans can be found canned and marinated in jars for immediate eating or simply soaked in brine for nibbling or adding to salads or other cold dishes.

NUTRITIONAL ANALYSIS

Calories:	258	
Protein:	20	g
Carbohydrates:	44	g
Dietary Fiber:	12	g
Fat:	1	g
Cholesterol:	0	mg
Sodium:	10	mg

Percent of Calories

Protein:	30%
Carbohydrates:	66%
Fat:	4%

PORTUGUESE BROAD BEAN SOUP WITH MINT

Serves 8

8 cups chicken stock
1 pound fresh broad beans
3 tablespoons olive oil
2 medium yellow onions, chopped
2 cloves garlic, chopped
2 medium potatoes, scrubbed and diced
2 teaspoons salt or to taste
½ teaspoon freshly ground black pepper or to taste
4 tablespoons minced fresh mint leaves

. . . .

1. Bring the chicken stock to a boil and add the beans. Simmer for 30 minutes, until the beans are tender.

2. Remove from the heat, drain, reserve the cooking liquor, and allow the beans to cool.

3. When the beans are cool enough to handle, remove and discard their shells. Slice the beans into thirds. Set aside.

4. Heat the olive oil in a sauté pan and sauté the chopped onions until they just begin to color. Add the chopped garlic and sauté for 1 minute more. Add the diced potatoes and continue cooking for 10 minutes longer.

5. Transfer the cooked onion and potato mixture to a blender or food processor container and process into a liquid, adding the reserved bean cooking liquor. Do this in batches. Return to the sauté pan and to the heat.

6. Add the cooked, sliced beans, season with salt and freshly ground black pepper, and bring the soup to a boil. Cook for 5 minutes, adjusting the consistency of the soup with additional water or stock if preferred.

7. To serve the soup, ladle into soup bowls and sprinkle with the minced mint leaves.

. . . .

Notes and Variations

One pound soaked dried broad beans can be used in place of the fresh. The potatoes can be peeled if you like; I prefer the skins in the soup. Fresh minced basil, dill, or chervil can be used in place of the mint.

. . . .

Lighter Version

Omit the olive oil and salt. Replace the regular chicken stock with nonfat, low-sodium chicken broth. Add 1 onion, ½ teaspoon black pepper, and 2 tablespoons mint.

NUTRITIONAL ANALYSIS

	Regular		Lighter Version	
Calories:	187		130	
Protein:	9.5	g	6	g
Carbohydrates:	21	g	26	g
Dietary Fiber:	4	g	5	g
Fat:	7	g	<1	g
Cholesterol:	0	mg	0	mg
Sodium:	1433	mg	130	mg

Percent of Calories

Protein:	21 %		19 %	
Carbohydrates:	46 %		78 %	
Fat:	33 %		3 %	

FRESH BROAD BEAN SOUP WITH POTATOES AND CORIANDER

Serves 8

5 *cups shelled fresh broad beans*

8 *cups chicken stock*

4 *medium potatoes, scrubbed and diced*

2 *medium onions, chopped*

¼ *cup chopped fresh cilantro leaves*

1 *teaspoon salt or to taste*

½ *teaspoon ground black pepper*

½ *cup fragrant green olive oil*

. . . .

1. In a soup pot, combine the shelled broad beans with the chicken stock, diced potatoes, chopped onions, and chopped cilantro leaves. Bring to a gentle simmer, cover, and cook for about 20 minutes, until the broad beans and diced potatoes are tender.

2. Carefully transfer the soup mixture to a blender or food processor container and process into a liquid. Do this in batches if necessary.

3. Return the mixture to the soup pot, season to taste with salt and freshly ground black pepper, and stir in the olive oil. Add more stock or water to thin the soup if desired.

4. Bring to a simmer and serve.

. . . .

Notes and Variations

This soup, which comes from Portugal, can be made with dried broad beans or fava beans. Use 1 pound and soak overnight — proceed from there. The cooking time will be longer. If the chicken stock is salted, be careful when you add salt. It is interesting that in this recipe the olive oil is added as a flavorant, not as a cooking medium. Be sure to use the most fragrant, the most fruity oil available.

Lighter Version

Omit the olive oil and salt. Substitute nonfat, low-sodium chicken stock for the regular chicken stock. Add an additional 2 tablespoons chopped fresh coriander just before serving.

NUTRITIONAL ANALYSIS

	Regular		Lighter Version	
Calories:	276		153	
Protein:	13	g	9.5	g
Carbohydrates:	30	g	29	g
Dietary Fiber:	6.5	g	6.5	g
Fat:	12	g	<1	g
Cholesterol:	0	mg	0	mg
Sodium:	1456	mg	699	mg

Percent of Calories

	Regular	Lighter Version
Protein:	19%	24%
Carbohydrates:	42%	73%
Fat:	39%	2%

EGYPTIAN BROAD BEAN SOUP WITH CUMIN AND LEMON

Serves 8

> 4 *cups dried broad beans, soaked for 48 hours*
>
> 10 *cups water*
>
> 2 *teaspoons ground cumin*
>
> 2 *teaspoons salt*
>
> 1 *teaspoon freshly ground black pepper*
>
> ½ *cup olive oil*
>
> 2 *tablespoons freshly squeezed lemon juice*
>
> ¼ *cup minced parsley*

1. Soak the dried broad beans for 48 hours, changing the water several times.

2. Drain, peel, and discard the skin from the soaked broad beans. Set the beans aside.

3. Combine the skinned broad beans in a soup pot with 10 cups water. Bring to a simmer, cover, and cook for 1 ½ hours, until the broad beans are very tender.

4. Transfer the beans and cooking liquor to a blender or food processor container and process into a liquid. Do this in batches. Return to the soup pot, adding more water if a thinner consistency is desired.

5. Season the soup with the ground cumin, salt, and freshly ground black pepper. Simmer for 2 minutes.

6. Stir in the olive oil and lemon juice.

7. To serve, ladle the soup into bowls and sprinkle with minced parsley.

. . . .

Notes and Variations

Use 6 cups fresh broad beans, when available, in place of the dried. You don't see broad beans served very much in the United States, at least not in restaurants. They are labor intensive and require the patience of an angel to peel the skins for an amount large enough to feed a family. But if you have the time, the result is worth it. This recipe comes from Egypt.

. . . .

Lighter Version

Omit the salt and olive oil. Add 1 teaspoon cumin, 2 tablespoons lemon juice, and ¼ cup minced parsley.

NUTRITIONAL ANALYSIS

	Regular		Lighter Version	
Calories:	379		262	
Protein:	20	g	20	g
Carbohydrates:	44.5	g	45	g
Dietary Fiber:	12	g	12	g
Fat:	15	g	1	g
Cholesterol:	0	mg	0	mg
Sodium:	554	mg	22	mg

Percent of Calories

Protein:	20 %	29 %	
Carbohydrates:	46 %	66 %	
Fat:	34 %	5 %	

PORTUGUESE FRESH BROAD BEAN SALAD

Serves 4

1 *quart water or to cover*
1 *pound fresh young broad beans, shelled*
¼ *cup olive oil*
2 *tablespoons lemon juice*
1 *clove garlic, minced*
1 *tablespoon chopped parsley*
1 *teaspoon salt or to taste*
½ *teaspoon freshly ground black pepper or to taste*

1. In a saucepan, bring enough water to cover the fresh broad beans to a boil and add the beans. Cook the beans at a boil for about 7 minutes, until tender to the bite. Drain the beans, transfer to a bowl, cover, and refrigerate.

2. When the beans are sufficiently chilled, add the olive oil, lemon juice, minced garlic, and parsley. Season to taste with salt and freshly ground black pepper and toss all together.

3. Cover the bowl and chill for another ½ hour or so before serving.

Notes and Variations

The cooking water can be salted. Balsamic vinegar makes a good replacement for the lemon juice. One tablespoon chopped fresh herbs can be added to the ingredients to expand the flavors of the salad: cilantro, oregano, basil, or mint. This salad can also be served warm or at room temperature.

Lighter Version

Omit the olive oil and salt. Add another tablespoon lemon juice, another clove garlic, and another tablespoon chopped parsley. One tablespoon of chopped fresh mint or basil can also be added.

NUTRITIONAL ANALYSIS

	Regular		Lighter Version	
Calories:	248		131	
Protein:	9	g	9	g
Carbohydrates:	23.5	g	24	g
Dietary Fiber:	6	g	6	g
Fat:	14	g	<1	g
Cholesterol:	0	mg	0	mg
Sodium:	539	mg	7	mg

Percent of Calories

Protein:	14 %	26 %
Carbohydrates:	37 %	71 %
Fat:	49 %	3 %

GREEK LAMB STEW
WITH FRESH BROAD BEANS

Serves 8

⅓ cup olive oil

1½ pounds lamb stew meat, cut into 1-inch cubes

2 medium onions, peeled and chopped

2 medium carrots, scraped and cut crosswise into thin rounds

2 ribs celery, stringed and chopped

4 medium tomatoes, skinned, seeded, and chopped

½ cup tomato paste

4 cloves garlic, peeled and chopped

1 cup dry red wine

4 cups water

1 teaspoon sugar

½ teaspoon ground cloves

4 bay leaves

½ cup chopped parsley

2 teaspoons salt or to taste

1 teaspoon freshly ground black pepper

2 pounds fresh young broad beans, rinsed

1. Heat the olive oil in a stew pot. Sauté the lamb cubes, turning to brown evenly on all sides.

2. Add the onions, carrots, chopped celery, tomatoes, tomato paste, and garlic. Cook together until the vegetables are nicely browned.

3. Add the red wine, water, sugar, ground cloves, bay leaves, and chopped parsley. Season with salt and freshly ground black pepper.

4. Bring to a boil, turn down to a very gentle simmer, cover, and cook for 45 minutes, until the lamb is tender.

5. Add the fresh broad beans, additional water if necessary, cover, and simmer another 30 minutes, until the beans are tender. Remove the bay leaves.

6. Adjust seasonings as desired and serve.

. . . .

Notes and Variations

Dried fava or broad beans are available always. Use 1 pound dry, soaked for 12 hours or more, in place of the fresh when not available. Dried beans need to be shelled after they are cooked tender. This same stew can be made with beef or pork.

. . . .

Lighter Version

Use only ½ pound lean lamb stew meat and omit the oil and salt. Add 4 cloves garlic and 4 bay leaves. Add an additional ¼ cup chopped parsley just before serving.

NUTRITIONAL ANALYSIS

	Regular		Lighter Version	
Calories:	377		203	
Protein:	30	g	14	g
Carbohydrates:	27	g	28	g
Dietary Fiber:	7	g	7	g
Fat:	15	g	3	g
Cholesterol:	69	mg	18	mg
Sodium:	1247	mg	685	mg

Percent of Calories

Protein:	31%	26%
Carbohydrates:	28%	52%
Fat:	36%	12%

SICILIAN BRAISED FAVA BEANS

Serves 6 as an appetizer or hors d'oeuvres

1	*pound dried fava beans, soaked overnight*
8	*cups water*
2	*medium yellow onions, chopped*
4	*medium tomatoes, coarsely chopped*
½	*cup tomato puree*
½	*cup chopped parsley*
1	*cup coarsely chopped celery*
2	*teaspoons salt or to taste*
1	*teaspoon freshly ground black pepper or to taste*
1	*teaspoon dried hot red pepper flakes*
6	*lettuce leaves for garnish*
¾	*cup grated Parmesan cheese*
½	*cup olive oil*

1. Rinse the soaked fava beans and transfer to a saucepan. Add water to cover, the chopped onions, chopped tomatoes, and tomato puree. Bring to a boil, reduce heat to a simmer, cover, and cook for 1½ hours, or until the fava beans are tender but not mushy. Add more water, if necessary, during cooking.

2. Transfer the fava beans to a bowl. Add the parsley, celery, and season with salt, black pepper, and dried red pepper flakes. Allow to cool to room temperature.

3. Line salad plates with a lettuce leaf and spoon the beans onto the leaves. Top the beans with 1 tablespoon grated Parmesan cheese per portion and sprinkle lightly with olive oil. Serve at room temperature.

4. The beans are to be eaten with the hands, squeezing the bean out of its skin into the mouth. The skins are discarded.

. . . .

Notes and Variations

This dish is messy and fun to eat. Don't forget hand towels or finger bowls. You can actually peel the fava beans for your guests, but this is a labor intensive process.

. . . .

Lighter Version

Omit the salt and olive oil. Reduce the measure of Parmesan cheese to ⅓ cup. Add 1 teaspoon of ground black pepper and ¼ cup chopped fresh oregano leaves.

NUTRITIONAL ANALYSIS

	Regular		Lighter Version	
Calories:	311		198	
Protein:	16	g	14.5	g
Carbohydrates:	32.5	g	32.5	g
Dietary Fiber:	8.5	g	9	g
Fat:	14	g	2	g
Cholesterol:	6	mg	2.5	mg
Sodium:	596	mg	93	mg

Percent of Calories

Protein:	20%	28%
Carbohydrates:	40%	63%
Fat:	40%	9%

EGYPTIAN FAVA BEAN PATTIES WITH GARLIC TAHINI

Serves 8 as an appetizer

    1   pound dried fava beans, soaked for 48 hours
    6   green onions, chopped
    ¼   cup chopped parsley
    2   tablespoons chopped cilantro
    4   cloves garlic, pressed
    2   teaspoons salt
    ½   teaspoon freshly ground black pepper
    ½   teaspoon cayenne pepper
    1   teaspoon baking soda
    2   cups sesame seeds
        Oil for frying
        Garlic Tahini Sauce (page 346)

1. Soak the fava beans in water for 48 hours, changing the water several times.

2. Drain and rinse the now plumped fava beans and skin them by squeezing them by an edge, hard enough for the bean to slip out of its skin. Discard the skins.

3. Process the fava beans into a dense pureed mass in a food processor or mash by hand.

4. Add the green onions, parsley, cilantro, pressed garlic, salt, black pepper, cayenne, and baking soda. Process again until all is well blended.

5. Roll the mixture into a ball, cover with a damp cloth, and set aside for 30 minutes to give the flavors time to develop throughout the bean mass.

6. Take the bean mass and pull it off by rounded tablespoonfuls and shape each piece into a patty approximately 1 ½ inches in diameter. As the patties are shaped, roll in the sesame seeds and place on a platter.

7. Heat about 2 inches of frying oil in a frying pan or skillet to 375°F. Carefully slip the patties into the hot oil without crowding the pan.

Fry them on one side for about 3 minutes, turn and fry on the other side for 2 minutes. They should be a deep golden brown.

8. With a slotted spoon, transfer the fava patties to a platter lined with absorbent paper and place in a warm oven. Repeat the frying process until all the patties are made.

9. Serve the fava bean patties alone or with a garlic tahini sauce for dipping.

. . . .

Notes and Variations

These patties can be served as an appetizer, side dish, or snack and can be served as hors d'oeuvres with cocktails, both hot and at room temperature. The garlic tahini is not absolutely necessary, but makes for a better dish. If you don't want to make the garlic tahini, squeeze some lemon juice over the patties. If you want the patties salty with cocktails, sprinkle more salt over them while they are still hot, just before serving.

. . . .

Lighter Version

Omit the salt. Instead of frying the patties, arrange them on a nonstick baking sheet and bake in a preheated 400°F oven for 12 minutes, until they are nicely browned and cooked all the way through. Add an additional 2 cloves garlic, another tablespoon chopped cilantro, and ½ teaspoon black pepper. Serve with the lighter version of lemon-garlic tahini (page 347).

NUTRITIONAL ANALYSIS

	Regular		Lighter Version	
Calories:	479		411	
Protein:	20	g	22	g
Carbohydrates:	42	g	44	g
Dietary Fiber:	12	g	13	g
Fat:	28	g	19	g
Cholesterol:	0	mg	0	mg
Sodium:	706	mg	173	mg

Percent of Calories

Protein:	16%	20%
Carbohydrates:	34%	41%
Fat:	50%	39%

East Chinese Sprouted Fava Bean Pâte

Serves 6 as an appetizer

1   *pound dried fava beans*
½   *cup red-in-snow (prepackaged Chinese vegetable)*
½   *cup Sichuan preserved vegetable (prepackaged)*
3   *cups water*
6   *tablespoons peanut oil*
1   *tablespoon sugar*
1   *cup rich chicken stock*
1   *tablespoon sesame oil*
½   *teaspoon salt or to taste*

. . . .

1. Rinse and pick over the fava beans and place them in a dish deep enough to just barely cover with water. Soak the fava beans, changing the water each day, for 4 days, until the beans have sprouted.

2. Drain the sprouted fava beans. Peel and discard the skins.

3. In a bowl, soak the red-in-snow in cold water for ½ hour, drain, and chop finely. Set aside.

4. Rinse the Sichuan preserved vegetable and chop it finely.

5. In a saucepan, combine the sprouted, skinned fava beans with the water. Cover and simmer gently for ½ hour, until the favas are very tender and the water is almost reduced completely.

6. Transfer the hot cooked fava beans to a food processor and process briefly into a coarse mash.

7. In a wok or skillet, heat 3 tablespoons of the peanut oil until it begins to smoke. Add the chopped red-in-snow and Sichuan preserved vegetable and stir-fry for 1 minute.

8. Add the fava bean mash, sugar, and ½ cup chicken stock. Stir and cook for 5 minutes.

9. Add the remaining peanut oil to the wok mixture as well as the remaining chicken stock. Add the sesame oil and adjust the salt if desired.

10. Transfer the mixture into a small loaf pan or soufflé dish, pressing it tightly. Cover and refrigerate for several hours, until completely cold.

11. To serve, turn the pâte out from the mold onto a plate and cut into slices.

. . . .

Notes and Variations

The red-in-snow and the Sichuan preserved vegetable are available prepackaged in Asian specialty markets. If these are not available, use prepackaged preserved cabbage, which is available in many supermarkets. If you like this dish, you may want to double the ingredients the next time.

. . . .

Lighter Version

Omit the salt. Reduce the peanut oil to 2 tablespoons. Replace the rich chicken stock with a nonfat, low-sodium chicken broth.

NUTRITIONAL ANALYSIS

	Regular		Lighter Version	
Calories:	417		334	
Protein:	20	g	20.5	g
Carbohydrates:	47	g	48	g
Dietary Fiber:	12.5	g	12.5	g
Fat:	17.5	g	8	g
Cholesterol:	<1	mg	0	mg
Sodium:	447	mg	131	mg

Percent of Calories

Protein:	19 %	24 %
Carbohydrates:	44 %	56 %
Fat:	37 %	21 %

LEBANESE FAVA BEAN AND CHICKPEA CROQUETTES *Serves 8 as an appetizer or side*

½ pound dried fava beans, soaked for 24 hours
½ pound dried chickpeas, soaked for 12 hours
   Water to cover
2 medium onions, chopped
6 cloves garlic, chopped
¾ cup chopped parsley
2 teaspoons baking soda
2 teaspoons ground coriander
1 teaspoon ground cumin
2 teaspoons salt or to taste
1 teaspoon freshly ground black pepper or to taste
1 teaspoon cayenne pepper
   Oil for deep frying
   Lemon-Garlic Tahini (page 347)

1. Peel the skins from the fava beans and rub the chickpeas together between your hands to loosen their skins. Discard the skins.

2. In a food processor, combine and process the fava beans and chickpeas with the chopped onions, garlic, parsley, and baking soda. Season with the coriander, cumin, salt, black pepper, and cayenne. Process the mixture into a homogeneous mass to make the croquette dough. Transfer the croquette dough to a floured surface and knead for 10 minutes. Allow to rest for ½ hour.

3. After the croquette mixture has rested, form it by breaking it off in pieces, about 1 tablespoon at a time, and shaping it into balls. Flatten the balls into thick patties. Allow to rest again for 30 minutes.

4. In a frying pan or skillet, heat a 1-inch depth of oil to 375°F. Add the croquettes without crowding the pan and fry in batches. Fry until richly brown on one side, about 3 minutes, turn and fry until the other side is browned, about 2 minutes more. With a slotted spoon or spatula, transfer the croquettes to an absorbent paper-lined platter and place in a warm oven until all the croquettes are made.

5. Serve hot with lemon-garlic tahini for dipping.

. . . .

Notes and Variations

This recipe can be made with 1 pound of either fava beans or chickpeas. The croquettes can be made larger and served as an entree. Aïoli sauce or simply freshly squeezed lemon juice also goes well with the croquettes.

. . . .

Lighter Version

Omit the salt. Bake the croquettes rather than frying them. Arrange the uncooked patties on a nonstick baking sheet. Allow to rest for 30 minutes. Bake in a preheated 375°F oven for 12 to 15 minutes, until they are nicely browned and cooked completely through.

NUTRITIONAL ANALYSIS

	Regular		Lighter Version	
Calories:	461		220	
Protein:	13.5	g	13.5	g
Carbohydrates:	38	g	38	g
Dietary Fiber:	9	g	9	g
Fat:	30	g	2.5	g
Cholesterol:	0	mg	0	mg
Sodium:	866	mg	333	mg

Percent of Calories

Protein:	12%	24%
Carbohydrates:	32%	66%
Fat:	56%	10%

LOUISIANA BOILED
FAVA BEANS

Serves 8 as an appetizer

1   *pound dried fava beans, soaked for 12 hours minimum*
6   *tablespoons liquid "crab boil"*
8   *cloves garlic, crushed*
1   *lemon, juiced*
1   *teaspoon sugar*
2   *tablespoons salt*

1. In a saucepan, combine the soaked fava beans with enough water to cover them by an inch. Add the liquid crab boil, garlic, lemon juice, and sugar and bring to a simmer. Cover and simmer gently for 2 hours, until the fava beans are just becoming tender.

2. Add the salt and boil for ½ hour more. At this point a cooled bean can be easily squeezed from its shell using the fingers.

3. Drain the beans and allow to cool.

4. Serve the fava beans at room temperature or chilled. Eat with the fingers, squeezing out the bean from its shell into your mouth, discarding the shell.

. . . .

Notes and Variations

Liquid crab boil is a product that we use in Louisiana to season the water in which we boil shellfish: crabs, shrimp, or crayfish. Replacements for this are seafood seasoning used in Maryland steamed seafood or even simply a bottle of pickling spice. They are all basically the same. You can flavor these boiled favas any way that you prefer: curry, chili, or cumin. These tasty little hors d'oeuvres are best served with cocktails or as snacks.

. . . .

Lighter Version

This recipe is already very healthful and only the omission of salt would improve its healthful benefits, reducing sodium content to 8 mg. Add the juice of another lemon to give the boiled favas a little more bite.

NUTRITIONAL ANALYSIS

Calories:	204	
Protein:	15	g
Carbohydrates:	35.5	g
Dietary Fiber:	9	g
Fat:	1	g
Cholesterol:	0	mg
Sodium:	360	mg

Percent of Calories

Protein:	29%
Carbohydrates:	67%
Fat:	4%

EAST CHINESE FAVA BEAN SPROUT SOUP

Serves 8

2 *cups sprouted fava beans*
½ *cup dried shrimp*
1 *cup boiling water*
2 *tablespoons peanut oil*
2 *teaspoons minced fresh ginger*
1½ *quarts rich chicken stock*
1 *cup diced preserved cabbage (condiment)*
1½ *tablespoons sesame oil*

1. Sprout the fava beans and remove and discard their skins.

2. In a small bowl, combine the dried shrimp with the boiling water and allow to soak for ½ hour or more. Drain the shrimp, reserving the soaking liquid.

3. In a saucepan or soup pot, heat the peanut oil and sauté the shrimp and minced ginger together for 1 minute.

4. Carefully pour in the chicken stock, the sprouted fava beans, and bring to a boil. Cover the saucepan, reduce to a gentle simmer, and cook for 12 minutes.

5. Add the diced preserved cabbage to the soup, along with the sesame oil. Cover and simmer for 5 minutes more.

. . . .

Notes and Variations

Fresh shrimp can be used in place of the dried. Use 1 ½ cups small peeled fresh raw shrimp to replace the dried shrimp. Fresh mung or soybean sprouts from the grocery will do in place of your having to sprout the favas yourself. And, in a pinch, canned sprouts can be used.

. . . .

Lighter Version

Omit the peanut oil. Add 1 additional teaspoon minced fresh ginger. Replace the rich chicken stock with nonfat, low-sodium chicken broth. Reduce the sesame oil to 2 teaspoons.

NUTRITIONAL ANALYSIS

	Regular		Lighter Version	
Calories:	101		41	
Protein:	6	g	3	g
Carbohydrates:	3	g	5	g
Dietary Fiber:	<1	g	<1	g
Fat:	7.2	g	1.5	g
Cholesterol:	10.5	mg	10.5	mg
Sodium:	719	mg	137	mg

Percent of Calories

Protein:	24 %		30 %	
Carbohydrates:	12 %		43 %	
Fat:	63 %		27 %	

CATALONIAN FAVA BEANS IN TOMATO SAUCE WITH CHORIZO

Serves 6

1   *pound dried fava beans, soaked overnight*

¼   *cup lard (traditional) or olive oil*

8   *ounces thick-cut smoked bacon, sliced crosswise into ½-inch-wide strips*

2   *large yellow onions, finely chopped*

6   *cloves garlic, minced*

4   *medium tomatoes, skinned, seeded, and chopped*

1   *cup dry white wine*

¼   *cup brandy or cognac*

1   *pound chorizo sausage, sliced into ¼-inch-thick rounds*

2   *tablespoons chopped fresh parsley leaves, plus 3 tablespoons for garnish*

1   *tablespoon chopped fresh mint leaves*

2   *teaspoons fresh thyme leaves*

2   *teaspoons chopped fresh oregano leaves*

1   *teaspoon salt or to taste*

1   *teaspoon freshly ground black pepper to taste*

2   *cups chicken stock*
    Water, if necessary

. . . .

1. Simmer the fava beans in water for 1½ hours, until tender. Shell the cooked fava beans and hold aside.

2. Cook the lard or olive oil and bacon together in a saucepan until the lard is rendered into liquid and the bacon is browned. Remove the bacon and set aside.

3. Add the chopped yellow onions to the rendered lard and bacon drippings and sauté until they just begin to color. Add the minced garlic, chopped tomatoes, dry white wine, brandy, and the shelled fava beans. Bring to a simmer, cover, and cook the favas in the sauce for 15 minutes to allow the sauce flavors to be absorbed by the favas.

4. Add the cooked bacon strips to the saucepan, along with the sliced chorizo sausage. Stir in the parsley, mint, thyme, and oregano. Season to taste with salt and freshly ground black pepper.

5. Add the chicken stock and enough water, if necessary, to cover the beans so that some are just barely exposed. Cover the saucepan and simmer for 15 minutes more.

6. Serve garnished with chopped parsley.

· ·

Notes and Variations

This dish is very hearty. The lard can be substituted with shortening or oil, but you won't get the distinctive richness of flavor that the lard imparts. Dried herbs can be used in place of the fresh: 1 teaspoon dried herbs to 1 tablespoon chopped fresh herbs.

· ·

Lighter Version

Many changes are necessary to make a lighter version of this very hearty rustic dish. It is nice to replace the meats here with mushrooms to give a flavor and texture apart from the fava beans themselves. Omit the lard, bacon, chorizo, salt, and chicken stock. Add 1 pound smoked turkey sausage, ½ pound turkey bacon, 1 tablespoon chopped fresh oregano, and nonfat, unsalted chicken stock.

NUTRITIONAL ANALYSIS

	Regular		Lighter Version	
Calories:	1122		584	
Protein:	41.5	g	40	g
Carbohydrates:	56	g	55	g
Dietary Fiber:	14	g	14	g
Fat:	77	g	19	g
Cholesterol:	113	mg	77	mg
Sodium:	1780	mg	784	mg

Percent of Calories

Protein:	15%		27%	
Carbohydrates:	20%		37%	
Fat:	61%		28%	

Soybeans

Soyabean, Soy Pea

Glycine max (or Glycine soja, Soja max)
ORIGIN: TROPICAL ASIA

Soybeans have been cultivated in tropical Asia for more than seven thousand years. The varieties exceed two thousand five hundred cultivars. They are widely grown now in East Asia, Europe, Brazil, and the United States.

Soybeans are eaten as immature pods, or fresh or dried as pulses. They are made into soy sauce, milk, cheese, tofu, meal, oil, and used as a coffee substitute.

There are more than one hundred varieties grown in the United States. With the development of the new soybean-based edible oil substitutes, soybeans will see an increase in cultivation.

Much of the Asian crop is made into condiments such as soy sauce, tamari, and fermented black bean paste.

EDAMAME, GREEN VEGETABLE SOYBEANS

A popular new addition to the soybean family recipe catalog in this country is the Edamame. Edamame is also called green vegetable soybean and is the green soybean that is cooked and eaten fresh or frozen like a pea. Edamame can be found fresh at specialty produce companies and Asian markets or in the frozen food section of health food stores. Try them in the many "pea" recipes in this book.

1 cup cooked green vegetable soybeans (removed from pod), no added salt or fat

Notes and Variations

The Edamame is exceptionally high in protein and can play an important role in a vegan or vegetarian regimen. Cook Edamame, or green vegetable soybeans, by removing the beans from the pods and boiling them in water for about 10 minutes or so, until tender. Use in salads, or season with salt and fresh herbs or butter and serve as you would fresh peas. Edamame is also popular steamed or boiled in the pod until tender, then served hot sprinkled with sea salt as an appetizer.

NUTRITIONAL ANALYSIS

Calories:	254	
Protein:	22	g
Carbohydrates:	20	g
Dietary Fiber:	7.5	g
Fat:	11.5	g
Cholesterol:	0	mg
Sodium:	25	mg

Percent of Calories

Protein:	33%
Carbohydrates:	29%
Fat:	38%

CLAMS IN SOY BEAN SAUCE

Serves 6 as an appetizer

Sauce

- 1½ cups cooked soybeans, pureed
- 1 cup chicken stock
- 3 tablespoons tamari or soy sauce
- 1½ tablespoons rice wine vinegar
- 1½ tablespoons dry sherry
- 1 tablespoon sesame oil
- 1 tablespoon minced fresh red chili pepper
- 1½ teaspoons sugar
- 1 teaspoon salt or to taste
- 3 pounds fresh clams in their shells
- 4 green onions, chopped, plus 1 green onion, chopped, for garnish
- 3 cloves garlic, chopped
- ¼ cup peanut oil

1. Prepare the soy bean sauce. In a small bowl, whisk the soy bean puree together with the chicken stock until smooth. Continue whisking as you add the soy sauce, rice wine vinegar, dry sherry, sesame oil, minced chili pepper, sugar, and salt. Set aside.

2. Clean the clams in their shells by brushing them under cold running water with a vegetable brush. Discard any partially opened clams.

3. Place the brushed clams in an unheated wok or wide frying pan. Add the chopped green onions, garlic, and peanut oil and cover the pan. Place on a moderate heat to begin cooking, shaking the pan from time to time to make sure there is a uniform cooking of the clams and a uniform opening of their shells.

4. When all the clams have begun to open, add the sauce mixture and bring to a boil. Simmer for about 2 minutes. Check for and discard any clams whose shells have not opened.

5. Transfer the clams and soy bean sauce to a serving dish and garnish with the chopped green onion.

· ·

Notes and Variations

The soy beans, dried or fresh, need only to be boiled until soft. Bottled clam juice from the grocer's shelf can be used in place of the chicken stock for a more intense clam taste. Or better, purchase your clams from a vendor who also supplies fresh clam juice. This dish can also be made with the same weight of small mussels or oysters. Three tablespoons of sherry wine vinegar can be used in place of the rice wine vinegar and sherry.

· ·

Lighter Version

Omit the peanut oil, salt, and sugar. Use low-fat, low-sodium chicken or other stock. Add ¼ cup chopped fresh cilantro to the finished recipe. Cook on a lower heat, stirring more often so nothing sticks to the wok.

NUTRITIONAL ANALYSIS

	Regular		Lighter Version	
Calories:	457		370	
Protein:	55	g	55	g
Carbohydrates:	17.5	g	17.5	g
Dietary Fiber:	1.8	g	1.8	g
Fat:	17.3	g	8	g
Cholesterol:	129	mg	129	mg
Sodium:	1113	mg	629	mg

Percent of Calories

Protein:	49 %	60 %	
Carbohydrates:	16 %	19 %	
Fat:	35 %	20 %	

CANTONESE SOYBEAN SNACKS

Serves 8 as an appetizer or hors d'oeuvres

1   *pound dried soybeans, soaked overnight*
8   *cups water*
½   *cup tamari*
¼   *cup dry sherry*
8   *slices ginger, the size of a quarter*
4   *tablespoons sugar*
4   *tablespoons plum sauce*
2   *tablespoons peanut oil*
2   *teaspoons salt or to taste*

. . . .

1. Rinse the soaked soybeans and put them in a saucepan with 8 cups water. Bring the water to a boil, cover, and turn down the heat to a slow simmer. Cook for 1 ½ hours, until the soybeans are tender yet retain a decided firmness.

2. Remove the cover from the pan and pour off all the water. Add the tamari, sherry, ginger, sugar, and plum sauce and continue cooking until all the liquid has reduced or been absorbed by the beans. Using a wooden spoon, carefully stir the soybeans around in the saucepan so that they are all evenly coated with the liquid as it dissipates.

3. Line a baking sheet with aluminum foil and grease with the peanut oil. Transfer the soybeans to the sheet in a single layer. Bake in a preheated 200°F oven for 1 hour. Turn off the oven and allow the soybeans to cool in the oven.

4. Sprinkle the soybeans with salt, if desired, and serve at room temperature.

. . . .

Notes and Variations

Port wine or Madeira can be used in place of the sherry. Chickpeas work well in this recipe. Hoisin sauce and Chinese rib sauce can replace the plum sauce.

NUTRITIONAL ANALYSIS

Calories:	268	
Protein:	19	g
Carbohydrates:	26	g
Dietary Fiber:	3.5	g
Fat:	11	g
Cholesterol:	0	mg
Sodium:	1076	mg

Percent of Calories

Protein:	27 %
Carbohydrates:	37 %
Fat:	35 %

CHINESE EGGPLANT BRAISED WITH SOYBEAN PASTE
Serves 6 as a side or appetizer

1½ pounds Japanese or regular eggplant
½ cup salt
    Peanut oil for deep frying
4 green onions, chopped
4 cloves garlic, pressed
2 teaspoons grated fresh ginger
½ cup packaged soybean paste
½ cup chicken stock
2 tablespoons soy sauce
2 tablespoons dry sherry
2 tablespoons sugar
1 tablespoon sesame oil

1. Skin the eggplant and cut into ¾-inch dice. Place on a plate in a single layer and sprinkle generously with salt. Cover the eggplant with plastic wrap and allow to stand for about ½ hour to sweat out the liquid. Rinse the eggplant dice with fresh water and pat dry with paper towels.

2. In a skillet or frying pan, heat a ½-inch depth of peanut oil to 350°F. Carefully add the eggplant dice, without crowding the pan, and fry, turning several times, until nicely browned on all sides. Using a slotted spoon, transfer the cooked eggplant to a plate lined with absorbent paper and set aside.

3. Pour off almost all of the frying oil except for a couple of tablespoons. Sauté the chopped green onions, garlic, and ginger for 1 minute.

4. Add the soybean paste and cook for 1 minute longer, stirring constantly.

5. Add the chicken stock, soy sauce, dry sherry, and sugar. Bring to a boil. Return the cooked eggplant to the pan, reduce the heat, cover, and cook until the eggplant is tender and the liquid is completely reduced.

6. Sprinkle the eggplant with sesame oil and serve.

. . . .

Notes and Variations

Soybean paste, packed in jars or cans, can be found in Asian markets or other specialty food stores. This recipe can also be made with zucchini or another fairly firm-fleshed squash.

. . . .

Lighter Version

Omit the peanut oil and cook the eggplant dice dry in a wide nonstick sauté pan or skillet. Replace the chicken stock with nonfat, low-sodium chicken broth. Reduce the sugar by 1 tablespoon and the sesame oil by 1½ teaspoons.

NUTRITIONAL ANALYSIS

	Regular		Lighter Version	
Calories:	194		95	
Protein:	5	g	4.5	g
Carbohydrates:	15.5	g	14	g
Dietary Fiber:	4	g	4	g
Fat:	13	g	3	g
Cholesterol:	0	mg	0	mg
Sodium:	866	mg	624	mg

Percent of Calories

	Regular	Lighter Version
Protein:	9 %	17 %
Carbohydrates:	31 %	53 %
Fat:	59 %	27 %

Peas

Green Pea, Garden Pea, Petits Pois, Sweet Pea, Field Pea, Dry Pea, Split Pea, Yellow Pea, Yellow Split Pea, Batani, Erbese, Ater, Pois, Takarmany, Borso, Marrowfat Pea, English Pea, Guisante

Pisum sativum
ORIGIN: MEDITERRANEAN TO IRAN

Pea, Edible-podded Sugar Pea, Chinese Pea

Pisum sativum
GROWN MOSTLY IN EUROPE AND THE ORIENT

Dun Pea, Grey Pea, Mutter Pea, Partridge Pea, Peluskins

Pisum sativum variety arvense
ORIGIN: MEDITERRANEAN TO IRAN

Sugar Pea, Mangetout

Pisum sativum variety macrocarpon
ORIGIN: MEDITERRANEAN

Peas are used universally in most world cuisines. Much of what is produced worldwide is processed fresh in cans and frozen, or dried. Flour is made from peas.

Peas are eaten as fresh green peas and the immature pods are eaten fresh, raw or cooked, as a vegetable, or used as an ingredient in countless international recipes. Rehydrated dried peas are used in place of fresh when fresh are not available.

Dried and split peas, whether green or yellow in color, are used worldwide in soups and other recipes that allow the peas to fairly dissolve into the resulting dish.

In Africa and Asia the tender greens and leaves of the plant are eaten as a vegetable. Peas are the most important processed vegetable in the United States and Britain.

Surprisingly, peas are becoming an important part of the snack market, where they are cooked in palm oil and salted or sweetened. Sometimes the peas are pureed, flavored, extruded into shapes, and cooked for another snack concept.

There are many varieties of peas, each with its own slight variation. They can all be prepared similarly. The preparation of peas begins as simply as eating them fresh from the pod, blanched or steamed, or even raw if they are tender young peas.

Low in fat, high in carbohydrate, with a 25 percent protein content, the pea is a valuable component of any regimen, especially where protein is less readily available such as in vegetarian diets.

NUTRITIONAL ANALYSIS

per ½ cup of raw fresh peas

Calories:	57	
Protein:	3.5	g
Carbohydrates:	10.5	g
Dietary Fiber:	3.7	g
Fat:	.1	g
Cholesterol:	0	mg
Sodium:	2	mg

Percent of Calories

Protein:	25 %
Carbohydrates:	73 %
Fat:	2 %

GREEN PEA AND CARROT SOUP WITH TAPIOCA

Serves 8

- 2 *tablespoons butter*
- 4 *shallots, chopped*
- 4 *cups fresh shelled green peas*
- 6 *cups water*
- 2 *large carrots, small dice*
- ¼ *cup instant tapioca*
- 1 *cup milk*
- 1 *teaspoon salt*
- ½ *teaspoon white pepper*
- 1 *cup sour cream*
- 4 *tablespoons chopped parsley*

. . . .

1. In a large saucepan, heat the butter and sauté the chopped shallots just until softened, about 2 minutes.

2. Add the peas and water, bring to a boil, turn down to a simmer, and cook until the peas are very soft, about 15 minutes. Liquefy the soup in a blender in batches and return to the saucepan.

3. Add the diced carrots, tapioca, milk, and season with salt and white pepper. Simmer until the carrots and tapioca are soft, about 6 minutes.

4. Add the sour cream. Bring to a simmer and cook for 5 minutes.

5. Adjust the seasonings to suit your taste, stir in the parsley, and serve.

Notes and Variations

A medium onion and 1 large clove garlic can be substituted for the shallots. The peas can be cooked from dried peas or from frozen or canned peas. Fresh will always make the best soup. If using canned, use the can liquid. It contains a great deal of flavor, but be careful with the addition of salt. There is salt in the canned peas and the liquid. If you don't use instant tapioca, cook it soft in boiling salted water, drain, and add to the soup. Other herbs can be added for another layer of flavor. Try oregano or rosemary.

Lighter Version

Omit the butter and salt. Replace the milk with skim milk and the sour cream with nonfat sour cream. Increase the chopped parsley by ¼ cup. Add 1 tablespoon of a fresh chopped herb such as rosemary or oregano when you add the parsley.

NUTRITIONAL ANALYSIS

	Regular	Lighter Version
Calories:	197	125
Protein:	6.5 g	6.8 g
Carbohydrates:	21 g	24 g
Dietary Fiber:	4.4 g	4.3 g
Fat:	10.3 g	<.5 g
Cholesterol:	24.7 mg	.5 mg
Sodium:	344 mg	50 mg

Percent of Calories

Protein:	13 %	22 %
Carbohydrates:	42 %	76 %
Fat:	46 %	2 %

BLACK FOREST
SPLIT GREEN PEA SOUP

Serves 6

   3   tablespoons butter
   2   medium onions, finely chopped
   2   carrots, chopped
   1   large rib celery, chopped
   1   large potato, scrubbed and diced
   2   smoked ham hocks
   6   cups water
   1   German beer
   1   pound dried split green peas, rinsed and drained
   1   tablespoon whole brown mustard seeds, crushed
1½   teaspoons dried thyme
   ¼   teaspoon ground clove
   3   links bratwurst, cut crosswise into ¼-inch-thick rounds
   2   teaspoons salt
   ½   teaspoon freshly ground black pepper
   2   tablespoons cider vinegar
   2   green onions, chopped
   ¼   cup chopped parsley

1. In a soup pot or large saucepan, melt the butter and sauté the chopped onions, carrots, and celery. Cook until the vegetables just begin to color.

2. Add the diced potato, smoked ham hocks, water, beer, split peas, crushed mustard seeds, thyme, and ground clove. Bring to a boil, reduce to a gentle simmer, cover, and cook, stirring occasionally, until the smoked ham hocks and split peas are very tender, about 2 hours.

3. Carefully lift the ham hocks from the soup and transfer to a plate. Remove the meat from the bones, dice, and return the diced meat to the soup. Discard the bones.

4. Add the bratwurst and simmer for 10 minutes more. Season to taste with salt and freshly ground black pepper.

5. Just a few minutes before serving, stir the cider vinegar, chopped green onions, and parsley into the soup.

. . . .

Notes and Variations

Two half-pickled pig's feet can be used in place of the ham hocks for a more tart flavor. Knockwurst works as well as the bratwurst. A good addition for extra flavor is a few tablespoons German mustard. Add more water in the cooking if the soup becomes too thick.

. . . .

Lighter Version

Omit the butter, bratwurst, and salt. (Or substitute a low-fat turkey sausage for the bratwurst.) Add the onions, carrots, and celery directly to the pot without precooking after the split peas have simmered for 1 hour. Continue simmering for another hour. Add an additional tablespoon crushed brown mustard seeds.

NUTRITIONAL ANALYSIS

	Regular		Lighter Version	
Calories:	578		408	
Protein:	31.5	g	26	g
Carbohydrates:	62	g	61	g
Dietary Fiber:	8	g	8	g
Fat:	22.5	g	6	g
Cholesterol:	59.5	mg	18.5	mg
Sodium:	1093	mg	86	mg

Percent of Calories

Protein:	21%	24%
Carbohydrates:	41%	58%
Fat:	34%	13%

Yellow Split Pea Soup with Italian Sausage

Serves 10

- 1 *pound split yellow peas*
- 10 *cups chicken stock*
- 2 *tablespoons olive oil*
- 5 *Italian sausage links*
- 2 *medium yellow onions, chopped*
- 1 *sweet green bell pepper, chopped*
- 4 *cloves garlic*
- 2 *tablespoons red wine vinegar*
- 1 *teaspoon oregano*
- 1 *teaspoon rosemary*
- 1 *teaspoon basil*
- 1 *teaspoon dried hot red pepper flakes*
- 2 *teaspoons salt or to taste*

1. Rinse the yellow split peas and put in a pot with the chicken stock. Bring to a rolling boil, turn down to a simmer, cover, and cook for 1 hour.

2. While the peas are cooking, heat the olive oil in a sauté pan and sauté the Italian sausages. Brown on all sides, puncturing on all sides with the tines of a fork or the tip of a small knife, to allow the fat and liquid to release in the cooking. When browned and cooked through, remove from the pan and allow to cool.

3. Add the chopped onions and bell pepper to the sauté pan and sauté until browned. Add the garlic and sauté for 1 minute more. Add to the split peas.

4. Slice the cooked Italian sausages into ½-inch-thick rounds and add to the peas.

5. Add the red wine vinegar, oregano, rosemary, basil, red pepper flakes, and season to taste with salt. Cover the pot and simmer gently for another hour, until the peas have reached the softness, or the soup the thickness, that you desire.

. . . .

Notes and Variations

This soup can be processed in a blender for a smooth texture. Another pork sausage of your preference can be used in place of the Italian sausage. Black pepper can replace the red pepper flakes, same measure. Any dried pea can be used in place of the yellow split peas. Add more chicken stock or water if the soup becomes too thick for your taste.

. . . .

Lighter Version

Omit the olive oil and salt. Replace the chicken stock with nonfat, low-sodium chicken broth. Use low-fat turkey sausage in place of the Italian sausage. Cook the turkey sausage and chopped onions dry in a pan, moving them around constantly so they don't stick and burn, until cooked. Cut up the sausage and add the sausage and onions to the peas. Add an additional ingredient of 2 teaspoons anise seeds.

NUTRITIONAL ANALYSIS

	Regular		Lighter Version	
Calories:	417		212	
Protein:	25	g	15.5	g
Carbohydrates:	32.5	g	35	g
Dietary Fiber:	4.5	g	4.5	g
Fat:	21	g	2	g
Cholesterol:	39	mg	11	mg
Sodium:	1738	mg	125	mg

Percent of Calories

Protein:	24%		28%	
Carbohydrates:	31%		63%	
Fat:	45%		9%	

BERLINOISE YELLOW SPLIT PEA SOUP

Serves 10

1	pound dried split yellow peas
12	cups water
4	ounces smoked bacon, diced
4	ounces smoked ham, diced
4	tablespoons butter
2	carrots, chopped
2	medium onions, chopped
1	large rib celery, chopped
2	cloves garlic, minced
4	tablespoons flour
2	medium potatoes, scrubbed and diced
1	teaspoon thyme
½	teaspoon marjoram
2	teaspoons salt or to taste
1	teaspoon freshly ground black pepper

1. In a large saucepan or soup pot, combine the split yellow peas with the water, and the diced smoked ham and bacon. Bring to a boil, reduce to a gentle simmer, cover, and cook for 1 hour, until the peas are soft.

2. In a sauté pan, melt the butter and sauté the chopped carrots, onions, celery, and garlic until they begin to color. Add the flour and continue cooking until the mixture is lightly browned. Add this vegetable mixture to the soup pot along with the diced potatoes, thyme, and marjoram.

3. Season to taste with salt and freshly ground black pepper. Simmer for 20 minutes and serve.

. . . .

Notes and Variations

You can use all ham or all bacon if you prefer. The potato is optional. This soup can be made with dried whole yellow or green peas.

. . . .

Lighter Version

Omit the bacon, butter, and salt. Replace the ham with a low-fat turkey or another ham and mince it rather than dicing it. Cook the carrots, onions, celery, and flour together in a dry pan, no butter or oil, stirring constantly so nothing sticks and burns. Cook until the mixture begins to color. Add to the soup pot and proceed. Increase the garlic by 2 cloves, the thyme by ½ teaspoon, and the marjoram by ½ teaspoon.

NUTRITIONAL ANALYSIS

	Regular	Lighter Version
Calories:	321	232
Protein:	16.5 g	15 g
Carbohydrates:	41.5 g	42 g
Dietary Fiber:	5 g	5 g
Fat:	10.5 g	1 g
Cholesterol:	24 mg	5 mg
Sodium:	738 mg	180 mg

Percent of Calories

Protein:	20 %	25 %
Carbohydrates:	51 %	70 %
Fat:	29 %	5 %

POTATO SALAD WITH GREEN PEAS AND GREEN BEANS

Serves 6

3 *medium potatoes, cooked*
1 *carrot, cooked*
1 *cup cooked green peas,*
1 *cup cooked green beans, cut into 1-inch lengths*
½ *cup finely chopped red sweet bell pepper*
2 *green onions, chopped*
2 *tablespoons chopped parsley*
1 *large clove garlic, pressed*
¾ *cup mayonnaise*
2 *tablespoons Dijon mustard*
1 *teaspoon salt or to taste*
¼ *teaspoon freshly ground black pepper*

1. Peel and dice the potatoes and the carrot.

2. Combine in a bowl with the green peas, green beans, bell pepper, green onions, chopped parsley, and pressed garlic.

3. Fold in the mayonnaise, mustard, and season to taste with salt and freshly ground black pepper.

4. Cover and refrigerate until ready to serve.

Notes and Variations

Leave the skins on the potatoes and get more flavor and nutrients. The bell pepper is red for the color; green bell pepper will produce as good a recipe. Increase or decrease the amount of mayonnaise to get the texture you prefer. Two chopped hard-boiled eggs are a good addition.

Lighter Version

Omit the salt. Replace the mayonnaise with nonfat mayonnaise. Increase the Dijon mustard by 1 tablespoon.

NUTRITIONAL ANALYSIS

	Regular		Lighter Version	
Calories:	304		129	
Protein:	4	g	4	g
Carbohydrates:	23	g	27	g
Dietary Fiber:	4	g	4	g
Fat:	23	g	<1	g
Cholesterol:	16	mg	0	mg
Sodium:	649	mg	410	mg

Percent of Calories

Protein:	5%	12%
Carbohydrates:	30%	81%
Fat:	65%	6%

HUNGARIAN GREEN PEA AND QUAIL SOUP

Serves 6

2 tablespoons butter

2 tablespoons bacon drippings

3 quail, cut into pieces for frying

2 carrots, cut into thin rounds

1 medium onion, chopped

3 tablespoons flour

6 cups hot chicken stock

2 cups shelled peas

1 cup mushrooms, quartered

2 teaspoons salt or to taste

½ teaspoon freshly ground black pepper or to taste

½ cup sour cream

2 tablespoons minced parsley

1. In a large saucepan or soup pot, heat the butter and bacon drippings and sauté the quail pieces until golden brown.

2. Add the chopped carrots, onion, and flour and continue cooking until the vegetables and flour begin to color.

3. Carefully whisk in the hot stock, being sure that no lumps remain in the flour-vegetable mixture. Simmer covered for 20 minutes, until the flesh of the quail is very tender.

4. Add the shelled peas, mushrooms, and season to taste with salt and freshly ground black pepper. Cook, covered, at a low simmer until the peas are tender, about 10 minutes.

5. To serve, stir in the sour cream and parsley and ladle into bowls.

Notes and Variations

Squab or Cornish hen or even chicken can be used in place of the quail. Add more stock if you find the soup too dense with ingredients. There is room here for the addition of another spice such as paprika or an herb such as tarragon or basil.

Lighter Version

Skin the quail and discard the skin and any visible fat. Omit the butter, bacon drippings, and salt. Cook the quail pieces, carrots, and onion in a dry pot, stirring constantly so they do not stick and burn. Add the flour and continue cooking and stirring for 3 minutes more before adding the chicken stock. Replace the regular chicken stock with nonfat, low-sodium chicken broth. Replace the sour cream with nonfat sour cream. Add another onion and 1 tablespoon cider vinegar when the stock is added.

NUTRITIONAL ANALYSIS

	Regular		Lighter Version	
Calories:	333		218	
Protein:	20	g	17	g
Carbohydrates:	16	g	23.5	g
Dietary Fiber:	3.5	g	4	g
Fat:	21	g	6.5	g
Cholesterol:	65	mg	41	mg
Sodium:	1603	mg	61	mg

Percent of Calories

Protein:	24%	30%
Carbohydrates:	19%	43%
Fat:	56%	27%

FRESH GREEN PEA AND LAMB STEW   *Serves 6*

1½ *pounds boneless lamb leg or shoulder, cut into 1-inch cubes*
1½ *teaspoons salt*
¾ *teaspoon white pepper*
3 *tablespoons butter*
3 *tablespoons vegetable oil*
6 *green onions, chopped*
3 *French shallots, minced*
2 *carrots, diced*
3 *cloves garlic, minced*
1 *cup dry white wine*
1½ *cups rich chicken stock*
6 *cups fresh shelled peas*
1½ *tablespoons chopped fresh mint leaves*

1. Season the cubed lamb lightly with ½ teaspoon salt and ¼ teaspoon white pepper.

2. Heat the butter and vegetable oil in a large saucepan and brown the seasoned lamb cubes.

3. Add the chopped green onions, French shallots, and diced carrots. Continue cooking until they begin to color.

4. Add the minced garlic and stir and cook for 1 minute more.

5. Add the white wine and chicken stock and bring to a boil. Turn down to a simmer, cover, and cook for 45 minutes, until the lamb is very tender.

6. Add the fresh shelled peas, cover, and simmer for another 8 minutes, until the peas are cooked.

7. Season to taste with 1 teaspoon salt and ½ teaspoon white pepper and add the mint just before serving.

Notes and Variations

Frozen or canned peas can be used in this recipe. Pork and heavy veal can be used in place of the lamb. Another oil of your preference can replace the vegetable oil. Beef or veal stock can be used in place of the chicken stock. Dried mint can be used in place of the fresh: use 1½ teaspoons. Or you can use dried rosemary leaves: 1½ teaspoons.

Lighter Version

Omit the butter, vegetable oil, and salt. Cook the lamb cubes dry in the pot. Move them around regularly while cooking to prevent sticking and burning while browning. Add the onions, shallots, carrots, and garlic and cook them dry, stirring constantly, until the onions become translucent. Replace the regular chicken stock with nonfat, low-sodium chicken broth. Add another clove garlic and another tablespoon fresh mint.

NUTRITIONAL ANALYSIS

	Regular		Lighter Version	
Calories:	448		332	
Protein:	33	g	32	g
Carbohydrates:	28.5	g	29	g
Dietary Fiber:	9	g	9	g
Fat:	19.5	g	7	g
Cholesterol:	88	mg	73	mg
Sodium:	863	mg	78	mg

Percent of Calories

Protein:	29 %		39 %	
Carbohydrates:	25 %		35 %	
Fat:	39 %		18 %	

CURRIED GREEN PEA AND LETTUCE SOUP

Serves 6

4   *tablespoons butter*
1   *large white onion, finely chopped*
3   *cloves garlic, finely chopped*
4   *tablespoons flour*
6   *cups chicken stock*
1½ *teaspoons curry powder*
1   *teaspoon ground turmeric*
1   *head butterhead or other lettuce, chopped*
2   *tablespoons lemon juice*
1   *teaspoon sugar*
2   *pounds fresh peas in pods, shelled*
1½ *cups hot scalded milk*
1   *teaspoon salt or to taste*
¼   *teaspoon freshly ground black pepper or to taste*

1. In a soup pot or saucepan, heat the butter and sauté the chopped onion and garlic until they just begin to color.

2. Blend in the flour and cook while stirring for 2 minutes. Whisk in the chicken stock.

3. Add the curry, turmeric, lettuce, lemon juice, sugar, and peas. Bring to a gentle simmer, cover, and cook for 10 minutes, until the peas are tender.

4. Stir in the hot milk and season with salt and freshly ground black pepper.

5. Liquefy the soup by carefully ladling it into a blender container in batches and processing on high speed.

6. Return to the pot to reheat and serve or refrigerate and serve chilled.

Notes and Variations

1 ½ pounds of peas in pods yields 2 cups shelled peas. Good quality frozen or canned peas can be used in place of the fresh. For a richer soup use heavy cream in place of the milk.

Lighter Version

Omit the butter and salt. Begin the cooking of the soup with the flour, which you must cook in a dry pan, stirring constantly until it acquires a beige color. Add the onion and garlic, cook while stirring for 2 minutes, slowly whisk in the chicken stock and proceed as above. Replace the regular chicken stock with nonfat, low-sodium chicken broth and the milk with skim milk. Add another clove garlic and an additional ½ teaspoon curry powder.

NUTRITIONAL ANALYSIS

	Regular		Lighter Version	
Calories:	197		124	
Protein:	11.5	g	7.5	g
Carbohydrates:	21	g	23	g
Dietary Fiber:	4	g	4	g
Fat:	8	g	<1	g
Cholesterol:	18.5	mg	1.1	mg
Sodium:	1206	mg	37	mg

Percent of Calories

Protein:	23%		24%	
Carbohydrates:	42%		72%	
Fat:	35%		4%	

FRESH PEAS WITH TUNA   *Serves 6 as an appetizer or side*

- 2   tablespoons light (yellow) olive oil
- 1   large onion, chopped
- 1   large tomato, skinned, seeded, and chopped
- 1   tablespoon tomato paste
- 4   cups shelled fresh green peas
- 2   tablespoons chopped parsley
- 1   tablespoon minced fresh oregano leaves
- 2   cloves garlic, minced
- ½   cup water
- ½   pound fresh tuna, cut into ½-inch dice
- 1   teaspoon salt or to taste
- ¼   teaspoon freshly ground black pepper or to taste

1. In a saucepan, heat the light olive oil and add the chopped onion, tomato, and tomato paste, cover, and simmer for 10 minutes.

2. Add the shelled fresh green peas, the chopped parsley, and the minced oregano and garlic. Add the water. Cover and simmer gently for 10 minutes, until the peas are tender.

3. Add the tuna dice to the peas, cover, and simmer for 5 minutes longer, until the tuna is cooked through.

4. Season with salt and freshly ground black pepper.

. . . .

Notes and Variations

Frozen or canned peas can be used in place of the fresh peas. Any fish can be used in this recipe, as well as canned tuna. 1 teaspoon dried oregano leaves can replace the 1 tablespoon fresh. Add more water if the mixture becomes too dry before the tuna is added to the peas.

. . . .

Lighter Version

Omit the olive oil and salt.
Add an additional tablespoon
tomato paste.

NUTRITIONAL ANALYSIS

	Regular		Lighter Version	
Calories:	193		155	
Protein:	15	g	15	g
Carbohydrates:	18.5	g	19	g
Dietary Fiber:	6	g	6	g
Fat:	7	g	2.5	g
Cholesterol:	14.5	mg	14.5	mg
Sodium:	401	mg	67	mg

Percent of Calories

Protein:	30 %	38 %
Carbohydrates:	38 %	48 %
Fat:	32 %	14 %

HUNGARIAN PEAS AND MASHED POTATOES

Serves 6 as a side

 2 *large potatoes, boiled soft*
 2 *tablespoons butter*
 1 *small onion, finely chopped*
 1 *small sweet red bell pepper, finely chopped*
 1 *tablespoon capers, finely chopped*
 6 *green olives, finely chopped*
 1 *tablespoon minced cornichon*
 ½ *cup milk*
 3 *cups cooked fresh green peas*
 1 *teaspoon salt*
 ¼ *teaspoon freshly ground black pepper*
 1 *tablespoon chopped parsley*

1. In a bowl, mash the boiled potatoes with their skins on. Set aside.

2. In a sauté pan, heat the butter and sauté the onion and bell pepper until the onion becomes translucent.

3. Add the capers, olives, and cornichon and sauté for 1 minute more.

4. Add the mashed potatoes and the milk and stir until smooth.

5. Carefully fold in the peas and season to taste with salt and freshly ground black pepper. Heat until all is hot.

6. Garnish with chopped parsley and serve hot.

Notes and Variations

You can skin the potatoes if you prefer them that way. If you don't have cornichon, any sour or dill pickle will suffice. Add more milk if you want the recipe looser. Fresh peas are rarely available in my neighborhood so I use frozen or canned peas in their place.

Lighter Version

Omit the butter and salt. Replace the whole milk with skim milk.

NUTRITIONAL ANALYSIS

	Regular		Lighter Version	
Calories:	183		144	
Protein:	6	g	6	g
Carbohydrates:	29	g	29	g
Dietary Fiber:	6	g	6	g
Fat:	5.5	g	<1	g
Cholesterol:	13	mg	.4	mg
Sodium:	597	mg	203	mg

Percent of Calories

Protein:	13%		17%	
Carbohydrates:	62%		79%	
Fat:	25%		5%	

Snow Peas

Sugar Pea, He Lan Dou, Kachang Puteh, Pattani Kadalai, Suet-Tau, Ho-Leng-Tau

Pisum sativum

ORIGIN: SOUTHEAST ASIA

Snow peas are a variety of the standard pea, garden pea, green pea. They are used at the immature green pod stage before the seeds within have had a chance to mature. The pod itself is more tender than most varieties of Pisum sativum.

The tender shoots of the plant are used as a vegetable and called "tou mio." The pods are also used after the seeds have grown to size, but are still tender. These are called sugar peas.

CHINESE STIR-FRIED SNOW PEAS AND VEGETABLES

Serves 6

12   dried black mushrooms
3   cups water
6   large leaves bok choy, rough chopped
     Water
⅓   cup peanut oil
1½   tablespoons minced fresh ginger
1   carrot, sliced crosswise into ⅛-inch rounds
3   ribs celery, rough chopped
6   water chestnuts, sliced into ⅛-inch rounds
1½   teaspoons sugar
1   pound snow peas, stringed
1   teaspoon salt
2   tablespoons soy sauce
2   teaspoons tapioca starch
2   tablespoons water

1. In a small bowl, soak the black mushrooms in water until sufficiently rehydrated and soft. Drain off and reserve ¼ cup of the soaking liquid. Trim off and discard any remaining tough parts and slice the mushrooms.

2. In a saucepan bring enough water to cover the chopped bok choy to a boil and blanch for 30 seconds. Drain.

3. Heat a wok over high heat until very hot and smoking. Add 4 tablespoons of the peanut oil. When the oil is hot, add the ginger and mushrooms. Stir-fry for 30 seconds.

4. Add the carrot rounds and ¼ cup of the reserved mushroom liquor. Cook until the liquid has dissipated.

5. Add the blanched bok choy, celery, and water chestnuts. Stir-fry for

1 minute and add the sugar and remaining peanut oil. Move the vegetable mixture to the side walls of the wok.

6. Add the snow peas to the bottom of the wok and season with the soy sauce.

7. Mix the tapioca starch with 2 tablespoons water and stir into the snow peas.

8. Mix all the ingredients together for another 30 seconds or so and serve.

. . . .

Notes and Variations

The mushrooms can be fresh or canned if you don't have dried. Other mushrooms can be used: oyster mushrooms, portobellos, shiitake, or straw. Fresh bean sprouts are a nice addition here. Cabbage can be used in place of the bok choy.

· ·

Lighter Version

Omit the peanut oil and salt. Add an additional tablespoon soy sauce. In a small bowl, soak the black mushrooms in the 3 cups water until sufficiently rehydrated and soft. Drain off and reserve 1 cup of the soaking liquid. Trim off and discard any remaining tough parts and slice the mushrooms. In a saucepan bring enough water to cover the chopped bok choy to a boil and blanch for 30 seconds. Add the reserved mushroom water to the wok and heat until the water boils vigorously. Add the ginger, mushrooms, and carrots and cover the wok. Steam over high heat for 5 minutes. Add the blanched bok choy, celery, and water chestnuts. Cover the wok and continue steaming the vegetables for 2 minutes. Add the sugar, snow peas, salt, and soy. Mix the tapioca starch with 2 tablespoons water and stir into the vegetables, cover the wok, and cook for 1 minute more. Serve hot with the pan liquid poured over.

NUTRITIONAL ANALYSIS

	Regular		Lighter Version	
Calories:	278		173	
Protein:	11	g	11.5	g
Carbohydrates:	31	g	31	g
Dietary Fiber:	7.5	g	7.5	g
Fat:	13	g	1	g
Cholesterol:	.2	mg	.2	mg
Sodium:	870	mg	734	mg

Percent of Calories

Protein:	16 %	25 %
Carbohydrates:	43 %	69 %
Fat:	41 %	5 %

STILTON SNOW PEAS

Serves 6 as an appetizer or hors d'oeuvres

Water to cover

3 *dozen snow peas, stemmed*

3 *ounces Stilton cheese*

2 *ounces cream cheese*

1 *tablespoon chopped parsley*

1 *teaspoon hot sauce (optional)*

1. Bring enough water to cover the snow peas to a boil and blanch the peas for 30 seconds. Transfer the peas to a colander and rinse under cool tap water to stop cooking. Drain and dry the snow peas.

2. In a small bowl, combine the Stilton, cream cheese, and parsley and work together with a few drops of hot sauce into a smooth homogeneous mass. Set aside.

3. Take the blanched dry snow peas and cut a 1-inch opening into the curved edge of each pea. Take a snow pea and hold it so that the cut is open. Using a teaspoon, fill the pea with the cheese mixture. Repeat the process until all the snow peas are filled.

4. Cover the peas with plastic wrap and chill before serving.

Notes and Variations

Blue cheese can replace the Stilton; it works just as well. A tablespoon or two of sherry added to the Stilton mixture enhances the flavor. Crushed walnuts, hazelnuts, or pecans give a nice extra flavor and crunchy texture — add ½ cup and overly stuff the pods.

Lighter Version

Change the cheese measures: use 1 ounce
Stilton, Roquefort, or blue cheese and
4 ounces nonfat cream cheese.

NUTRITIONAL ANALYSIS

	Regular		Lighter Version	
Calories:	93		42	
Protein:	4	g	4.5	g
Carbohydrates:	2	g	2.5	g
Dietary Fiber:	.5	g	.5	g
Fat:	7.5	g	1.5	g
Cholesterol:	23	mg	5.5	mg
Sodium:	285	mg	178	mg

Percent of Calories

Protein:	18 %		42 %	
Carbohydrates:	8 %		25 %	
Fat:	74 %		32 %	

Black-Eyed Peas

Cowpea, Crowder Pea, Southern Pea, Field Pea, Callivance, Cherry Bean, Frijol, China Pea, Indian Pea, Cornfield Pea, Niebe, Pois à Vaches, Haricot Indigène, Augenbohne, Costeño, Fríjol de Costa, Rabiza

Vigna sinensis
ORIGIN: INDIA, MIDDLE EAST

Black-eyed peas and crowders are most often used in good country or Southern cooking. Sometimes referred to as pea beans, they are used in various world cuisines where they are often referred to simply as peas, not to be mistaken for garden peas, Pisum sativum.

This type of "pea" is more closely related to the beans (Phaseolus) than to the peas (Pisum). Several slightly differing types are grown as black eye, brown eye, cream peas or cream crowders, Louisiana cream pea, differing in the size and color markings on the seeds.

Pods are 3 to 12 inches long and slender. Seeds are small, 1/6 to 1/4 inch in length. The peas are harvested at several stages of growth: as immature green pods, at the green-shell stage while pods are still green, or as dried peas threshed from the dry pods.

The whole immature pod with the beans intact is consumed prepared as for any green bean, snap bean, or string bean. The "pea" is shelled and eaten fresh, prepared as for any bean or pea, and the dry "pea" or bean is cooked as any dried bean or pea.

BLACK-EYED PEA SOUP WITH SMOKED HAM HOCKS

Serves 8

1   *pound dried black-eyed peas*
8   *cups water*
2   *smoked ham hocks*
2   *tablespoons oil*
2   *tablespoons all-purpose flour*
1   *large onion, chopped*
2   *ribs celery, finely chopped*
1   *teaspoon salt*
1   *teaspoon black pepper*
¼   *teaspoon cayenne pepper*

1. Rinse the black-eyed peas and combine with the water in a bean pot with the smoked ham hocks. Bring to a simmer, cover, and cook for about 1½ hours, until the peas become tender.

2. Remove the ham hocks to a cutting board or plate. Cut out and discard the bones. Dice the meat and return it to the peas.

3. In a sauté pan, heat the oil and stir in the flour. Cook while stirring for about 3 minutes, until the mixture acquires an off-white or amber color. Add the chopped onion and celery and sauté until they begin to color. Add to the bean pot.

4. Season to taste with salt, black pepper, and cayenne.

Notes and Variations

Black-eyed peas do not have to be presoaked before cooking like dried beans. The ham hocks usually lose most of their fat during the smoking process. Most of the remaining flesh is high protein. The hocks are usually salt-cured before smoking. Remember this when adding additional salt. This simple recipe can be embellished with bay leaves or garlic. The thickness of the soup can be adjusted by the addition of water or stock.

Lighter Version

Omit the oil, flour, and salt. Replace the ham hocks with ½ pound low-fat ham. Add ¼ cup chopped fresh parsley at the end of cooking.

NUTRITIONAL ANALYSIS

	Regular		Lighter Version	
Calories:	356		238	
Protein:	24	g	19	g
Carbohydrates:	38	g	36.5	g
Dietary Fiber:	6.5	g	6.5	g
Fat:	12.5	g	2	g
Cholesterol:	39	mg	13	mg
Sodium:	408	mg	432	mg

Percent of Calories

Protein:	27%	32%
Carbohydrates:	42%	60%
Fat:	31%	8%

PORTUGUESE BLACK-EYED PEA SALAD

Serves 6

- 1 *pound black-eyed peas, soaked overnight*
- 2 *quarts water*
- 1 *tablespoon salt*
- 2 *medium yellow onions, minced*
- 2 *cloves garlic, pressed*
- ⅓ *cup green virgin olive oil*
- 2 *tablespoons white wine vinegar*
- ¼ *cup chopped parsley*
- ½ *teaspoon freshly ground black pepper*
- 6 *lettuce leaves*

1. In a saucepan, combine the black-eyed peas, water, and salt and bring to a boil, turn down to a simmer, cover, and cook for 1 hour, until the peas become tender yet remain firm to the bite. Drain the black eyes and transfer to a bowl. Cover the bowl and refrigerate.

2. When the peas are sufficiently chilled, add the minced onions and pressed garlic, olive oil, white wine vinegar, and chopped parsley. Season with freshly ground black pepper. Adjust salt if desired. Re-cover the bowl and chill for another ½ hour or so to allow the flavors to meld.

3. Serve the salad on lettuce leaves.

Notes and Variations

Red onions would serve nicely here in place of the yellow for a milder, sweeter taste. The oil used should be fruity with the bouquet of fresh olives. Other vinegars will work. Try balsamic vinegar or malt vinegar.

Lighter Version

Omit the 1 tablespoon salt in the cooking water and don't salt the completed salad to taste. Omit the olive oil as part of the dressing. Add 2 cloves pressed garlic, ¼ cup vinegar, ¼ cup chopped parsley, and ½ teaspoon black pepper.

NUTRITIONAL ANALYSIS

	Regular		Lighter Version	
Calories:	387		287	
Protein:	19	g	19	g
Carbohydrates:	52	g	54	g
Dietary Fiber:	9	g	9	g
Fat:	13	g	1	g
Cholesterol:	0	mg	0	mg
Sodium:	1089	mg	25	mg

Percent of Calories

Protein:	19 %	25 %
Carbohydrates:	52 %	71 %
Fat:	30 %	3 %

BRAZILIAN BLACK-EYED PEA FRITTERS

Serves 8 as an appetizer or side

1   *pound black-eyed peas, soaked overnight*
½   *cup water or more*
2   *medium onions, chopped*
2   *cloves garlic, chopped*
2   *teaspoons salt*
½   *teaspoon black pepper*
1   *quart peanut oil for frying*
6   *limes*
    Habanero pepper sauce (approximately 2 teaspoons per serving)

1. Soak the black-eyed peas overnight, drain, and rinse. Take the peas by the handful and rub them together in your hands over a bowl to remove their skins. Discard the skins.

2. In a blender or food processor, puree the peas with the water into a thick paste; use more water if necessary. Add the chopped onions, garlic, and salt and freshly ground black pepper to taste. Process again until all the ingredients are well pureed.

3. In a deep fryer or heavy skillet, heat 2 inches of oil to 375°F. Using a tablespoon, scoop up the seasoned black-eyed pea paste and carefully slip it into the hot oil. Work quickly to put as many tablespoons of the paste at a time in the hot oil without overcrowding the skillet. Fry until nicely browned on one side, about 2 minutes, turn over and fry on the other side for about 1 minute longer, until browned.

4. Using a slotted spoon, transfer the fritters to a plate lined with absorbent paper. Hold the fritters in a warm oven until all the black-eyed pea paste is used.

5. Serve with limes and hot sauce as a condiment.

. . . .

Lighter Version

Omit the salt. Rather than fry the fritters in oil, the fritters can be oven-baked on a nonstick baking sheet at 400°F for about 12 minutes, until nicely browned. Add an additional 2 cloves chopped garlic and ½ teaspoon black pepper to the paste.

NUTRITIONAL ANALYSIS

	Regular		Lighter Version	
Calories:	356		222	
Protein:	11	g	14	g
Carbohydrates:	33	g	43	g
Dietary Fiber:	6	g	8	g
Fat:	21	g	<1	g
Cholesterol:	0	mg	0	mg
Sodium:	371	mg	12	mg

Percent of Calories

Protein:	12 %		24 %	
Carbohydrates:	36 %		73 %	
Fat:	52 %		3 %	

BRAZILIAN POACHED BLACK-EYED PEA CAKES

Serves 6

1 *pound black-eyed peas, soaked overnight and drained*
2 *tablespoons palm kernel oil*
2 *ounces dried shrimp, peeled whole or ground*
1 *medium yellow onion, finely chopped*
2 *teaspoons salt or to taste*
1 *teaspoon habanero pepper sauce or to taste*
3 *banana leaves*
1 *quart water*
2 *tablespoons salt*

. . . .

1. Simmer the black-eyed peas in water until they are soft, about 1½ hours. Drain.

2. Place the black-eyed peas in the container of a food processor and process into a smooth paste.

3. Add the palm kernel oil, shrimp, finely chopped yellow onion, salt, and habanero pepper sauce. Process all ingredients together. Set aside.

4. Prepare the banana leaves by cutting out six 8-inch squares and plunging them into boiling salted water to blanch and make them more pliable.

5. Lay the banana leaf squares flat on a surface. Place one-sixth of the black-eyed pea filling onto the top banana leaf square, folding the leaf up from each side to form a square, completely covering the filling. Tie the packet around one way, then the other, with cotton string to hold it closed in the poaching. Repeat this process for each leaf.

6. In a large saucepan, bring the water to a boil and add the salt. When boiling, add the packets to the water and poach for about 10 minutes, until they float to the surface.

7. Remove the cakes from the poaching water, drain, remove the cotton strings, and serve hot or at room temperature.

Notes and Variations

Palm kernel oil is known as dende in Brazilian Portuguese and can be found in specialty markets. The cakes can be made into an even more smooth texture by rubbing the soaked black-eyed peas together in your hands to remove their skins, which are then discarded. Limes and more hot sauce can be served as condiments. Other greens can be used if you don't have banana leaves; try cabbage, collards, mustard or turnip greens. Use enough to completely cover the pea filling and tie the leaves around the filling accordingly.

Lighter Version

For a lighter version, omit the palm kernel oil and salt. Replace the medium onion with a large one. Add one or more teaspoons habanero sauce, according to your taste.

NUTRITIONAL ANALYSIS

	Regular		Lighter Version	
Calories:	352		316	
Protein:	24	g	25	g
Carbohydrates:	53	g	53	g
Dietary Fiber:	11	g	11	g
Fat:	6	g	1.6	g
Cholesterol:	41	mg	41.5	mg
Sodium:	779	mg	69	mg

Percent of Calories

Protein:	27 %	30 %
Carbohydrates:	58 %	65 %
Fat:	15 %	5 %

BLACK-EYED PEAS WITH HAM

Serves 6 as an entree

 1   *pound black-eyed peas*
 8   *cups water*
 2   *bay leaves*
 ½   *pound smoked ham*
 1   *tablespoon bacon drippings*
 1   *large onion, chopped*
 1   *clove garlic, minced*
 ½   *teaspoon dried thyme leaves*
 ¼   *teaspoon ground sage*
 2   *teaspoons salt*
 1   *teaspoon black pepper*

1. Combine the black eyes, water, and bay leaves in a saucepan and bring to a gentle simmer. Dice the ham into ½-inch cubes and add to the peas. Cover and cook for 1 hour. Remove the bay leaves.

2. Heat the bacon drippings in a pan and sauté the chopped onion and garlic until they begin to brown. Add to the peas.

3. Add the thyme, sage, and season to taste with salt and pepper.

4. Simmer gently for 30 minutes more, until the peas are very tender.

Notes and Variations

The seasoning can be your choice. In this most basic of recipes, ham is used. Other seasoning meats can be used: salt pork, pickled pork, bacon, tasso, or almost any sausage. The bacon drippings can be replaced with lard (traditional) or a noncholesterol oil such as olive oil or peanut oil. Add more onion, garlic, and bay leaves if you like. Season with cayenne in the cooking or with hot sauce at the table. Serve the black-eyed peas over hot fluffy rice for a more complete entree.

Lighter Version

Omit the bacon drippings and salt. Replace the ham with low-fat pork ham or low-fat turkey ham. Increase the garlic measure to 3 cloves and the bay leaf count to 4. Double the thyme and sage measures. Add 1 teaspoon Louisiana hot sauce to the peas at the end of cooking.

NUTRITIONAL ANALYSIS

	Regular		Lighter Version	
Calories:	328		302	
Protein:	25	g	24.5	g
Carbohydrates:	47.5	g	48	g
Dietary Fiber:	8.5	g	8.5	g
Fat:	5	g	2	g
Cholesterol:	18	mg	18	mg
Sodium:	1112	mg	464	mg

Percent of Calories

Protein:	30%	32%
Carbohydrates:	57%	62%
Fat:	13%	6%

BLACK-EYED PEAS WITH PICKLED PIGS' TAILS

Serves 6 as an entree

1 *pound black-eyed peas*
1 *pound pickled pigs' tails*
8 *cups water*
4 *tablespoons lard or bacon drippings*
1 *large onion, chopped*
1 *large sweet green bell pepper, chopped*
4 *cloves garlic*
1 *teaspoon dried thyme leaves*
2 *teaspoons salt*
1 *teaspoon black pepper*
¼ *teaspoon cayenne pepper*
1 *tablespoon red wine vinegar*
3 *tablespoons chopped parsley*
3 *tablespoons chopped green onion*
6 *cups hot fluffy white rice (see rice analysis)*

1. Put the black eyes and pickled pigs' tails in a pot with the water and bring to a boil. Turn down to a simmer, cover, and cook for 1 hour.

2. Heat the lard in a skillet and sauté the onion, bell pepper, and garlic until they are nicely browned. Add to the black eyes along with the thyme, salt, black pepper, cayenne, and vinegar. Simmer, covered, for another 30 minutes, until very tender.

3. To serve, spoon the black eyes and pigs' tails on hot fluffy cooked rice and garnish with parsley and green onion.

. . . .

Notes and Variations

Smoked ham hocks can replace the pickled pigs' tails. The black eyes can be served alone, without the rice. Another rice can be used — brown, Arborio, jasmine. Any oil of your preference can replace the lard.

. . . .

Lighter Version

Omit the lard and salt. Use 1 smoked ham hock in place of the pound of pigs' tails. When the ham hock is tender, debone, mince the meat, and return to the black eyes. Add 2 cloves garlic, 1 teaspoon thyme, and 1 tablespoon red wine vinegar.

NUTRITIONAL ANALYSIS

	Regular		Lighter Version	
Calories:	598		305	
Protein:	40	g	21	g
Carbohydrates:	50	g	51	g
Dietary Fiber:	9	g	9	g
Fat:	27	g	3	g
Cholesterol:	90	mg	9	mg
Sodium:	967	mg	43	mg

Percent of Calories

Protein:	26%		27%	
Carbohydrates:	33%		65%	
Fat:	40%		9%	

Chickpeas

Garbanzo, Ceci, Channa, Pois Chiche,
Yellow Gram, Spanish Pea, Bengal Gram,
Hommes, Hamaz, Nohud, Lablabi,
Shimbra, Hiyoko Mame

Cicer arietinum

ORIGIN: TURKEY, WESTERN ASIA

Chickpea is the world's third largest pulse crop. Archaeological evidence show that chickpeas were first domesticated in the Middle East as early as seven thousand years ago and were widely cultivated in India, the Mediterranean area, the Middle East, and Ethiopia since antiquity. Brought to the New World, it is now important in Mexico, Argentina, Chile, Peru, and the United States, where it is extensively grown in California. It is also important in Australia and is also grown in Latin America where it is called garbanzo. In Italy it is called ceci.

The pea is called chickpea because it resembles a chick's head. The seedpod contains one to two peas. The chickpea is slightly larger than a pea. It has an irregular round shape, buff colored, with a texture that is firm and a mild, nutlike flavor.

The whole or ground seed is used in many ways by Mediterranean cultures and is also gaining popularity in America. Chickpeas are eaten fresh as green vegetables, boiled, fried, and roasted. In the Middle East they are used in sweets and condiments; seeds are ground and the flour can be used as soup, dhal, and to make bread; prepared with pepper, salt, and lemon it is served as a side dish. Dhal is the split chickpea without its seed coat, dried and cooked into a thick soup or ground into flour for snacks and sweetmeats. Sprouted seeds are eaten as a vegetable or added to salads. Chickpea is used roasted like peanuts and as a coffee substitute. Young plants and green pods are eaten like spinach. A small proportion of canned chickpea is also used in Turkey and Latin America, and to produce fermented food.

Chickpea is used extensively in India, the Mediterranean, and Italy, where it is often used in minestrone. In Mexico it is a commonly used dried pea. It is also fast becoming more popular in the United States, particularly in the West and Southwest.

Chickpea is the most hypocholesteremic agent of all peas, beans, and lentils, called pulses. Acids from the chickpea are considered beneficial in lowering blood cholesterol levels.

ANDALUCIAN CHICKPEA AND TRIPE STEW

Serves 8 as an entree

1   *pound dried chickpeas, soaked*

2   *pounds beef tripe, cut into 1-inch squares*

10   *cups water*

1   *cup lard (traditional) or olive oil*

4   *slices stale white bread, or stale French bread to equal same*

4   *chorizo sausages, cut crosswise into ½-inch-thick rounds*

1   *cup ground or pounded walnuts*

8   *tablespoons paprika*

2   *large yellow onions, chopped*

8   *cloves garlic, chopped*

6   *large tomatoes, peeled, seeded, and chopped*

¼   *teaspoon ground cloves*

4   *bay leaves*

1   *tablespoon salt*

2   *teaspoons freshly ground black pepper*

1. In a Dutch oven or covered saucepan, combine the soaked chickpeas, tripe, and water, bring to a boil, turn down to a simmer, and cover. Cook for 1 hour. After an hour, the chickpeas and the tripe should begin to tenderize.

2. In a sauté pan or skillet, heat half of the lard and fry the stale bread on both sides to a golden brown. Transfer the bread to a plate and crush it completely into crumbs.

3. Add the remaining lard and fry the chorizo sausage rounds for about 2 minutes.

4. Add the pounded walnuts and paprika and cook for 2 minutes longer.

5. Add the chopped onions and garlic to the sauté pan with the sausages and sauté all together for 3 minutes more.

6. Add the chopped tomato and cook all together for 5 minutes, until the mixture begins to thicken.

7. Add the sausage mixture to the chickpea and tripe, along with the ground cloves and bay leaves. Season to taste with salt and freshly ground black pepper. Simmer for another hour, until the chickpeas and tripe are tender and the sauce has reduced to a thick stew consistency. Remove the bay leaves.

Notes and Variations

If you are not a fan of tripe, you can replace it with the same measure of veal, beef, chicken, turkey, beef heart, or kidney. Though lard is the traditional fat used in this recipe, you may want to change the fat to a light olive oil. This is a truly rich and hearty dish, especially appealing to tripe lovers. Tripe is a marvelous product, distinctively flavored and textured, virtually fat and cholesterol free and very high in protein. This dish comes from the roving Spanish and Portuguese gypsy bands.

Lighter Version

Omit the lard and salt. Increase the ground cloves from ¼ to ½ teaspoon, the bay leaves from 4 to 8, and the black pepper from 2 teaspoons to 1 tablespoon.

NUTRITIONAL ANALYSIS

	Regular		Lighter Version	
Calories:	851		624	
Protein:	41	g	41	g
Carbohydrates:	58	g	59	g
Dietary Fiber:	11	g	11	g
Fat:	52	g	27	g
Cholesterol:	158	mg	134	mg
Sodium:	1362	mg	564	mg

Percent of Calories

Protein:	19 %	26 %
Carbohydrates:	27 %	37 %
Fat:	54 %	38 %

CHICKPEA AND CRAYFISH CAKES

Serves 8 as an entree

1 pound dried chickpeas, soaked
6 green onions, chopped
4 cloves garlic, minced
1 teaspoon dried thyme leaves
2 teaspoons salt
½ teaspoon freshly ground black pepper
½ teaspoon cayenne pepper or to taste
2 eggs, lightly beaten
6 tablespoons lemon juice
1 pound crayfish tail meat and fat if available
2 cups bread crumbs
1½ sticks butter (12 tablespoons)
¼ cup chopped parsley

1. Rinse and pick over the chickpeas and soak in 2 quarts water overnight.

2. Rub the soaked chickpeas between your hands to remove their skins. Discard the skins.

3. In a food processor, process the chickpeas into a dense mass. Add the chopped green onions, minced garlic, thyme, salt, black pepper, and cayenne. Process in the beaten eggs and 2 tablespoons lemon juice. Transfer the mixture to a bowl and fold in the crayfish tails and fat.

4. Divide the mixture into 16 parts and form into patties or cakes. Roll the cakes in the bread crumbs and arrange on a plate until ready.

5. In a wide skillet or frying pan, melt 1 stick butter until it is hot and fry the cakes in batches, first on one side for 2 minutes, then on the other for about 1 minute. They should be golden brown and cooked completely through. As the cakes are cooked, transfer them to a warm plate and hold in a warm oven.

6. When they are all cooked, add the remaining lemon juice to the pan with the remaining butter to deglaze the pan, and pour the pan juices over the cakes.

7. Serve garnished with chopped parsley.

. . . .

Notes and Variations

Half butter and half vegetable oil may work better for you as a frying medium; it cooks hotter without burning than butter alone. Shrimp or crabmeat work well in place of the crayfish. Try serving these cakes with a dipping sauce: hummus, aïoli, or cocktail sauce.

. . . .

Lighter Version

Omit the crayfish fat, salt, egg yolks, and butter. Add 2 egg whites. Don't fry the cakes. Arrange on a baking sheet and bake in a preheated 400°F oven for 15 minutes, until golden brown and cooked all the way through.

NUTRITIONAL ANALYSIS

	Regular	Lighter Version
Calories:	538	375
Protein:	26.5 g	26.5 g
Carbohydrates:	56 g	56 g
Dietary Fiber:	8.5 g	8.5 g
Fat:	24 g	3.7 g
Cholesterol:	175 mg	75.5 mg
Sodium:	1004 mg	307 mg

Percent of Calories

Protein:	19%	28%
Carbohydrates:	41%	59%
Fat:	40%	13%

PORTUGUESE CHICKPEA AND SALT COD SALAD

Serves 6 as an entree salad

 1 pound dried chickpeas, soaked
 8 cups water
 1½ pounds salt cod, soaked overnight in cool running water
 1 large onion, chopped
 2 cloves garlic, minced
 4 hard-boiled eggs, diced
 2 tablespoons chopped parsley
 2 teaspoons paprika
 ¼ teaspoon cayenne pepper
 ¾ cup olive oil
 ¼ cup cider vinegar
 2 teaspoons salt or to taste
 1 teaspoon freshly ground black pepper

1. Combine the chickpeas and water and bring to a boil. Turn down to a simmer, cover, and cook for 1½ hours, until the chickpeas are tender yet still somewhat firm to the bite. Do not cook them soft.

2. In another saucepan or sauté pan, combine the salt cod with enough water to cover and bring to a boil. Turn down to a simmer and cook for about 20 minutes, until the fish has rehydrated and is fairly tender. Drain the fish and cool. Break it apart into bite-sized pieces, discarding any remaining bones.

3. In a bowl, combine the cooked chickpeas with the salt cod pieces. Fold in the chopped onion, minced garlic, chopped hard-boiled eggs, and chopped parsley. Add the paprika, cayenne, olive oil, and cider vinegar. Season with salt and freshly ground black pepper.

4. Serve lukewarm.

Notes and Variations

This salad is served lukewarm, but can also be served chilled. This Portuguese dish relies on salt cod as a principal ingredient. It can be made, however, with fresh cod or another fish of your choice. Try snapper, grouper, or shark: steam, sauté or grill the fish before breaking up and adding to the salad. This salad can be made with virtually any dried bean in place of the chickpeas.

Lighter Version

Omit the yolks of the hard-boiled eggs, oil, and salt. Add 2 hard-boiled egg whites, 2 teaspoons paprika, 2 tablespoons chopped parsley, ¼ teaspoon cayenne, and ¼ cup cider vinegar. Remember that the sodium remains high; the cod is salt-preserved.

NUTRITIONAL ANALYSIS

	Regular		Lighter Version	
Calories:	909		619	
Protein:	90.5	g	89.5	g
Carbohydrates:	50	g	48	g
Dietary Fiber:	10	g	8.3	g
Fat:	38	g	7	g
Cholesterol:	314	mg	172	mg
Sodium:	8741	mg	8088	mg

Percent of Calories

Protein:	40%		57%	
Carbohydrates:	22%		32%	
Fat:	38%		11%	

JORDANIAN CHICKPEA
CABBAGE ROLLS

Serves 8 as an appetizer

1	*cup olive oil*
8	*green onions, chopped*
1½	*cups cooked white rice*
2	*cups cooked chickpeas*
2	*cups chopped tomatoes*
½	*cup minced parsley*
½	*teaspoon ground allspice*
3	*teaspoons salt or to taste*
1	*teaspoon freshly ground black pepper or to taste*
	Water to cover
32	*large raw cabbage leaves*
4	*cloves garlic, pressed*
2	*tablespoons minced fresh mint leaves*
6	*tablespoons freshly squeezed lemon juice*

1. In a sauté pan or skillet, heat 1 cup olive oil and sauté the chopped green onions until limp. Transfer the cooked green onions to a bowl and add the cooked rice, cooked chickpeas, chopped tomatoes, minced parsley, and allspice and season with 2 teaspoons salt and freshly ground black pepper. Set aside.

2. Fill a soup pot with enough water to completely cover the cabbage leaves when added. Bring to a boil and blanch the leaves in boiling water until pliable. Carefully remove the tender leaves to drain.

3. When the leaves are cool enough to handle, lay them out one by one and cut out the remaining stiff middle rib of each leaf. Arrange these removed ribs to line the fireproof-covered baking dish or casserole that you will use to cook the cabbage rolls.

4. Take the trimmed cabbage leaves and in the center of each place a rounded tablespoon of the chickpea and rice stuffing. Roll up the leaves as you go, folding in the sides first to hold in the filling. Arrange the

cabbage rolls in the baking dish.

5. In a small bowl, combine the pressed garlic with 1 teaspoon salt, mint, lemon juice, and ½ cup olive oil. Pour the mixture over the cabbage rolls in the baking dish. Add water, just enough to barely cover the cabbage rolls. Cover the baking dish.

6. Place the baking dish on the stove top and bring to a very gentle simmer. Simmer for about ¾ hour. Remove from the heat.

7. Serve hot or at room temperature.

. . . .

Notes and Variations

1 teaspoon crumbled dry mint leaves can be used in place of the fresh. Other large greens can be used in place of the cabbage such as collard or turnip greens. The pan liquor can be made into a sauce to serve over the cabbage rolls. After the rolls are removed, reduce the pan liquor by half and thicken with a few teaspoons cornstarch.

. . . .

Lighter Version

Omit the olive oil and the first step and simply add the green onions to the rice with the other ingredients. Omit the remaining salt and the remaining olive oil. Add ½ teaspoon allspice, 2 cloves garlic, 2 tablespoons mint, and 4 tablespoons lemon juice.

NUTRITIONAL ANALYSIS

	Regular		Lighter Version	
Calories:	420		184	
Protein:	8	g	8	g
Carbohydrates:	37	g	37	g
Dietary Fiber:	13	g	13	g
Fat:	29	g	2.3	g
Cholesterol:	0	mg	0	mg
Sodium:	1015	mg	215	mg

Percent of Calories

Protein:	7%	15%
Carbohydrates:	33%	74%
Fat:	60%	10%

CHICKPEA FISH NUTS

Makes 6 cups

1   *pound dried chickpeas, soaked*
8   *cups water*
¼   *cup peanut oil*
2   *tablespoons Asian fish sauce or to taste*
2   *teaspoons salt or to taste*

. . . .

1. Boil the chickpeas in plain water until tender, but not too much so. Drain and allow to dry.

2. Heat the peanut oil in a wide sauté pan or skillet and add the cooked chickpeas. Sauté the chickpeas for 5 minutes, until they have a golden color.

3. Sprinkle in the fish sauce and season with salt. Stir or shake to coat all the chickpeas evenly. Cover and sauté for about 30 seconds longer, until all the liquid in the pan is completely absorbed.

4. Transfer to a dish and serve hot or at room temperature.

. . . .

Notes and Variations

Fish sauce is an unthickened solution made from water, anchovies, and salt. It is used in much the same way as soy sauce is to flavor foods. This simple little recipe is a grand idea. Replacing nuts with chickpeas as a snack or cocktail appetizer substantially reduces fats. These "nuts" can also be used in salads and as a garnish for other vegetable dishes. If you are an aficionado of fish sauce, use more of it and less salt. You can also replace the fish sauce with soy sauce or teriyaki sauce.

. . . .

Lighter Version

Omit the salt and peanut oil. Heat the cooked chickpeas in a dry sauté pan with the fish sauce. Even though the fish sauce is high in sodium, the result is more healthful in fat and sodium content.

NUTRITIONAL ANALYSIS

	Regular	Lighter Version
Calories:	217	169
Protein:	9.5 g	9.5 g
Carbohydrates:	27.5 g	27.5 g
Dietary Fiber:	5.4 g	5.4 g
Fat:	8.2 g	2.8 g
Cholesterol:	2 mg	2 mg
Sodium:	709 mg	283 mg

Percent of Calories

	Regular	Lighter Version
Protein:	17 %	22 %
Carbohydrates:	50 %	64 %
Fat:	33 %	14 %

CHICKPEA GARLIC AND PARSLEY NUTS

Serves 6 as an appetizer

1 *pound dried chickpeas, soaked*
8 *cups water*
¼ *cup olive oil*
4 *large garlic cloves, pressed*
¼ *cup minced parsley*
2 *teaspoons salt or to taste*

. . . .

1. Cook the chickpeas in the water until tender. Drain and allow to dry.

2. Heat the olive oil in a sauté pan or skillet and add the cooked chickpeas. Sauté the chickpeas for 5 minutes, until they have a golden color.

3. Add the pressed garlic, minced parsley, and season with salt. Shake the sauté pan to coat all the chickpeas evenly. Cover and sauté for about 30 seconds longer, until all the liquid in the pan is completely absorbed.

4. Transfer to a dish and serve hot or at room temperature.

. . . .

Notes and Variations

Another fresh minced herb can be used in place of the parsley; try basil, mint, dill, or chives. Serve with cocktails or eat as a snack in place of chips or peanuts. Store in a covered container in the refrigerator for up to 2 weeks.

. . . .

Lighter Version

Omit the olive oil and salt.
Add 2 tablespoons red wine vinegar.

NUTRITIONAL ANALYSIS

	Regular		Lighter Version	
Calories:	215		167	
Protein:	9	g	9	g
Carbohydrates:	28	g	28	g
Dietary Fiber:	5.5	g	5.5	g
Fat:	8	g	2.5	g
Cholesterol:	0	mg	0	mg
Sodium:	438	mg	12	mg

Percent of Calories

	Regular	Lighter Version
Protein:	16 %	20 %
Carbohydrates:	51 %	65 %
Fat:	33 %	14 %

CURRIED GARBANZO NUTS   *Serves 8 as an appetizer or hors d'oeuvres*

1   *pound dried chickpeas, soaked*
¼   *cup olive oil*
1   *tablespoon salt*
1   *teaspoon curry powder*

1. Simmer the soaked garbanzo beans for an hour or until tender to the bite, but still slightly firm. Drain the water from the pot.

2. Fold in the olive oil, working the garbanzos gently to get them all covered with the oil without breaking them up.

3. Season the cooked garbanzos with the olive oil, salt, and curry powder. Fold the seasoning in carefully.

4. Heat the garbanzos stirring from time to time until they begin to color. Remove from the heat.

5. Serve hot or at room temperature with cocktails or as a snack.

Notes and Variations

Refrigerate the garbanzos in a covered container and eat as snacks instead of chips or nuts. Use as a garnish for salads, soups, or other hot and cold vegetable dishes, and for curry dishes. Spice them up with a hot pepper sauce.

. . . .

Lighter Version

Omit the olive oil and salt.
Add ¼ cup cider vinegar and 1 teaspoon
hot pepper sauce to taste.

NUTRITIONAL ANALYSIS

	Regular		*Lighter Version*	
Calories:	268		209	
Protein:	11	g	11	g
Carbohydrates:	35	g	35	g
Dietary Fiber:	7	g	7	g
Fat:	10	g	3.5	g
Cholesterol:	0	mg	0	mg
Sodium:	813	mg	14	mg

Percent of Calories

Protein:	16 %	20 %
Carbohydrates:	50 %	65 %
Fat:	34 %	15 %

GARBANZO AND SALT COD BRANDADE

Serves 6 as an entree

1 *pound salt cod*
½ *pound garbanzo beans, soaked*
6 *cups water*
12 *new potatoes*
Water to cover
¼ *cup olive oil*
3 *green onions, chopped*
2 *tablespoons chopped parsley*
4 *large cloves garlic, minced*
1 *small rib celery, chopped*
¼ *teaspoon white pepper or to taste*
¼ *teaspoon cayenne pepper or to taste*
2 *tablespoons fresh lemon juice*
1 *egg, lightly beaten*
1 *cup bread crumbs*
Aïoli (optional), garlic mayonnaise

1. Soak the salt cod overnight in a bowl under a thin stream of running water to flush the salt of the fish out of the soaking water.

2. Simmer the garbanzo beans for 1 hour, until tender to the bite. Drain off and discard the water.

3. Bring enough water to cover the new potatoes to a boil and boil the potatoes for 40 minutes, until tender enough to mash. Drain off the water and mash the potatoes in the pot, tearing up the skins as you work. Hold aside.

4. Put the cod in another pan with enough water to cover and bring it to a boil. Turn down to a simmer and cook until it is tender and can

be flaked apart, about 15 minutes. Remove and discard any skin or bones. Flake the flesh apart.

5. In a bowl or electric mixer, work the potatoes and codfish together until they become a dense mass.

6. In a skillet or frying pan, heat the olive oil and add the chopped green onions, chopped parsley, minced garlic, celery, white pepper, and cayenne. Sauté until they begin to color.

7. Add the codfish-potato mash. Stir and cook until the mash begins to color slightly. Squeeze in the lemon juice and remove from the heat.

8. When the mixture is cooled slightly, fold in the garbanzos and the beaten egg to complete the brandade mixture.

9. Oil a baking dish and sprinkle with bread crumbs. Add the brandade. Bake in a 375°F oven for 30 minutes, until the top crust is golden and a knife blade pierced into the center of the mixture comes out clean.

10. Serve hot or at room temperature, either plain or with aïoli.

. . . .

Notes and Variations

Because of the salt that will remain in the cod, even after soaking and simmering, be cautious in adding additional salt. Fresh cod can be used in place of the salt cod. Any white fleshy fish is good here. Cooked, skinned fava beans can be used in place of the garbanzos. Extra lemon on the side or a freshly made tartar sauce is good.

· ·

Lighter Version

Replace the salt cod with fresh. Omit the olive oil and salt. Use 2 egg whites in place of the whole egg. Add 3 green onions, 2 tablespoons chopped parsley, 2 cloves garlic, 1 rib celery, and 2 tablespoons lemon juice.

NUTRITIONAL ANALYSIS

	Regular		Lighter Version	
Calories:	511		277	
Protein:	57	g	24	g
Carbohydrates:	37	g	38.5	g
Dietary Fiber:	5	g	5.5	g
Fat:	14	g	3	g
Cholesterol:	146	mg	32.5	mg
Sodium:	5477	mg	220	mg

Percent of Calories

Protein:	46%	34%
Carbohydrates:	29%	56%
Fat:	25%	10%

GARLIC AND BASIL CHICKPEA TART

Serves 8 as an appetizer

1   *pound dried chickpeas, presoaked*
8   *cups water*
2   *teaspoons salt*
½   *cup garlic cloves, sliced paper thin*
½   *cup chopped fresh basil leaves*
½   *teaspoon freshly ground black pepper or to taste*
2   *tablespoons fruity olive oil*

1. Boil the chickpeas in the water until very tender, but not yet mushy. Drain the chickpeas, reserving the cooking liquid.

2. In a food processor, combine the cooked chickpeas and 1 teaspoon salt and process into a thick doughlike mass, adding some of the cooking liquid if necessary. The resulting mass must be dense enough to hold its shape.

3. Place the chickpea mass on a floured surface and mash or roll it out into a circle, about ½ inch thick. Line the top of the tart with the thinly sliced garlic and sprinkle with the chopped basil leaves. Season with 1 teaspoon salt and freshly ground black pepper. Sprinkle on the olive oil.

4. Bake the chickpea tart in a preheated 375°F oven for 30 minutes, until the edges are browned.

5. Cut the tart into 8 slices and serve hot.

Notes and Variations

This marvelous replacement for dough can be topped in any number of ways — try sun-dried tomatoes and Parmesan cheese or smoked salmon and cream cheese. The recipe is nice served with grated Romano or Parmesan cheese on the side.

Lighter Version

Omit the salt and olive oil.
Add 1 tablespoon dried hot red pepper flakes and 2 tablespoons chopped fresh oregano leaves.

NUTRITIONAL ANALYSIS

	Regular		Lighter Version	
Calories:	241		212	
Protein:	11.2	g	11.2	g
Carbohydrates:	35.5	g	35.6	g
Dietary Fiber:	6.9	g	6.9	g
Fat:	6.8	g	3.5	g
Cholesterol:	0	mg	0	mg
Sodium:	547	mg	15	mg

Percent of Calories

Protein:	18%		21%	
Carbohydrates:	57%		65%	
Fat:	25%		14%	

IRANIAN PULSE AND BARLEY SOUP WITH LAMB

Serves 6

1	*pound boneless lamb shoulder, cut into 1-inch cubes*
½	*cup chickpeas, soaked*
½	*cup red beans, soaked*
8	*cups water*
¾	*cup pearl barley, rinsed*
½	*cup brown lentils, rinsed*
2	*teaspoons salt or to taste*
1	*teaspoon freshly ground black pepper or to taste*
2	*cups chopped spinach, well washed*
4	*green onions, chopped*
½	*cup chopped parsley*
2	*tablespoons minced fresh cilantro leaves*
2	*tablespoons minced fresh mint leaves*
1	*teaspoon turmeric*
2	*tablespoons butter*
1	*large onion, chopped*

1. Combine the lamb in a soup pot with the soaked chickpeas and red beans. Add the water and bring to a gentle simmer, cover, and cook for 1 hour.

2. Add the barley and lentils to the simmering beans and lamb. Season with salt and freshly ground black pepper, bring to a gentle simmer, cover, and cook for another hour or more, until the beans are tender and the lamb is very tender, even shredding.

3. Add the chopped spinach, green onions, parsley, cilantro, mint, and turmeric. Cover and simmer for 5 minutes more.

4. In a small sauté pan, heat the butter and sauté the chopped onion until it is nicely browned. Adjust the seasonings if desired.

5. To serve the soup, ladle into bowls and garnish with the sautéed onion.

Notes and Variations

Pulse is the name used for all dried beans and peas. Other combinations of beans, peas, or lentils can be used. Pork could replace the lamb. More water can be added if the soup becomes too thick. A chicken, veal, or beef stock can replace all or part of the water for a richer soup.

Lighter Version

Omit the lamb and salt and the butter at the end of cooking. Add 2 tablespoons each of mint and cilantro and replace the water with a nonfat, low-sodium chicken, veal, or beef stock.

NUTRITIONAL ANALYSIS

	Regular		Lighter Version	
Calories:	453		349	
Protein:	26.5	g	20	g
Carbohydrates:	53	g	65	g
Dietary Fiber:	12	g	15	g
Fat:	16	g	2	g
Cholesterol:	58	mg	0	mg
Sodium:	824	mg	33	mg

Percent of Calories

Protein:	23 %	22 %
Carbohydrates:	46 %	73 %
Fat:	31 %	5 %

Israeli Chickpea Falafel Croquettes

Serves 6 as an entree

2 cups boiling water
1 cup bulgur wheat
1 pound dried chickpeas, soaked
4 cloves garlic, pressed
¼ cup chopped parsley
2 teaspoons baking powder
½ cup all-purpose flour
2 teaspoons ground coriander
2 teaspoons ground cumin
½ teaspoon cayenne pepper
½ cup freshly squeezed lemon juice
1 tablespoon salt or to taste
1 teaspoon freshly ground black pepper
Oil for deep frying

1. Pour the boiling water over the bulgur in a bowl and allow to soak for 10 minutes. Drain off the water completely.

2. In a food processor, combine the chickpeas, garlic, and parsley. Process briefly. Add the bulgur, baking powder, flour, coriander, cumin, cayenne, lemon juice, salt, and black pepper. Process into a smooth doughlike mass.

3. Break off the dough into pieces the size of a small egg, approximately 24, and shape into balls. When all the dough is used, cover the balls with a damp cloth and allow to rest for ½ hour.

4. In a frying pan or skillet, heat about 2 inches of oil to 350°F. Fry the falafel, turning during the process, until they become a rich golden brown, about 5 minutes. With a slotted spoon, transfer the cooked falafel to an absorbent paper-lined platter and hold in a warm oven until all are done.

5. Serve while still quite hot.

· ·

Notes and Variations

These croquettes can be served as an appetizer or side as well as an entree. Salt and/or lemon juice can be sprinkled over the falafel before serving. Serve with a dipping sauce like hummus or garlic tahini.

· ·

Lighter Version

Simply omit the salt. Don't fry the falafel in oil, but bake on a nonstick baking sheet at 350°F for 15 to 20 minutes, until they rise and are nicely browned. Serve with a lighter version of garlic tahini.

NUTRITIONAL ANALYSIS

	Regular		Lighter Version	
Calories:	425		304	
Protein:	14	g	14	g
Carbohydrates:	56	g	56	g
Dietary Fiber:	11	g	11	g
Fat:	17.5	g	4	g
Cholesterol:	0	mg	0	mg
Sodium:	942	mg	143	mg

Percent of Calories

Protein:	13 %		18 %	
Carbohydrates:	51 %		71 %	
Fat:	36 %		11 %	

MEXICAN CHICKPEA NUTS

Makes 6 cups, eighteen ⅓-cup servings

1 *pound dried chickpeas, soaked*
8 *cups water*
1 *tablespoon salt*
1 *stick butter*
6 *cloves garlic, pressed*
1 *tablespoon chili powder*
2 *teaspoons Coleman's dry mustard*
1 *teaspoon ground cumin*
½ *teaspoon cayenne pepper*

1. Combine the chickpeas and the water in a saucepan and bring to a boil. Boil gently for 1 hour. Add the salt and boil for ½ hour more. Drain and hold the chickpeas aside.

2. Melt the butter in a skillet and sauté the cooked chickpeas until they begin to color.

3. Add the pressed garlic, chili powder, dry mustard, ground cumin, and cayenne. Cook, while stirring, for 2 to 3 minutes. Remove from the heat.

4. Serve hot or cold with additional salt sprinkled over, if desired.

Notes and Variations

These are great replacements for peanuts or snack foods such as potato chips. Make your own variations as you like.

. . . .

Lighter Version

Omit the salt and butter. Combine all the ingredients in a saucepan and add ½ cup fresh lime juice. Heat and stir until all the lime juice is absorbed.

NUTRITIONAL ANALYSIS

	Regular	Lighter Version
Calories:	144	101
Protein:	5.3 g	5.3 g
Carbohydrates:	16.1 g	16.7 g
Dietary Fiber:	3.2 g	3.3 g
Fat:	7 g	2 g
Cholesterol:	13.8 mg	0 mg
Sodium:	420 mg	13 mg

Percent of Calories

	Regular	Lighter Version
Protein:	14 %	20 %
Carbohydrates:	43 %	63 %
Fat:	43 %	17 %

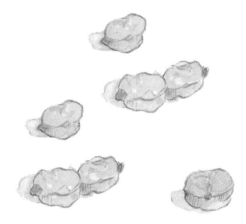

MIDDLE-EASTERN CHICKPEA
HUMMUS DIP

Yield: 1 quart, sixteen 1/4-cup servings

- 1 *pound dried chickpeas, soaked*
- 8 *cups water*
- 4 *cloves garlic, pressed*
- 2 *tablespoons fresh lemon juice*
- 6 *tablespoons sesame tahini*
- ½ *teaspoon ground cumin*
- 1 *teaspoon salt or to taste*
- 2 *tablespoons minced parsley*

1. Boil the chickpeas in the water until tender. Drain. Reserve the cooking water.

2. Combine the cooked chickpeas, garlic, lemon juice, sesame tahini, cumin, salt, and minced parsley. Process in a food processor or blender, adding the reserved cooking water a little at a time until the consistency of the sauce is smooth and thick, yet pourable.

3. Serve as a dip with raw vegetables or crisp toasted pita strips.

Notes and Variations

I developed this recipe with the intention of it being quite healthy and good from the start. There is no lighter version.

NUTRITIONAL ANALYSIS

Calories:	124	
Protein:	5.8	g
Carbohydrates:	16.6	g
Dietary Fiber:	3.5	g
Fat:	4.4	g
Cholesterol:	0	mg
Sodium:	127	mg

Percent of Calories

Protein:	18 %
Carbohydrates:	51 %
Fat:	30 %

ASIAN CHICKPEA NUTS

Serves 8 as an appetizer

4 *tablespoons peanut oil*
1 *tablespoon sesame oil*
1 *pound dried chickpeas, soaked, cooked tender and drained*
½ *teaspoon Chinese mixed spice*
2 *teaspoons salt or to taste*

1. In a sauté pan, heat the peanut and sesame oils and add the cooked chickpeas. Sauté the chickpeas until they are golden.

2. Add the Chinese mixed spice and salt and shake the sauté pan to coat all the chickpeas evenly. Cover and sauté for about 30 seconds longer, until all the liquid in the pan is completely absorbed.

3. Transfer to a dish and serve hot or at room temperature.

Notes and Variations

Any powdered spice can be used in place of the Chinese mixed spice. Other oils can also be used to create different flavors. These "nuts" are best served with aperitifs before dinner or as a snack.

. . . .

Lighter Version

Omit the peanut oil and salt.
Add 1 ½ teaspoons Chinese mixed spice.

NUTRITIONAL ANALYSIS

	Regular		Lighter Version	
Calories:	268		209	
Protein:	10.5	g	10.5	g
Carbohydrates:	32	g	32.5	g
Dietary Fiber:	6	g	6	g
Fat:	11.5	g	5	g
Cholesterol:	0	mg	0	mg
Sodium:	541	mg	9	mg

Percent of Calories

Protein:	15 %		19 %	
Carbohydrates:	47 %		61 %	
Fat:	38 %		20 %	

ROMAN CHICKPEA SOUP

Serves 8

1   *pound chickpeas, soaked*

1   *cup olive oil*

2   *teaspoons rosemary*

4   *cloves garlic, minced*

6   *anchovy fillets, chopped*

2   *tablespoons tomato paste*

2   *cups water*

2   *teaspoons salt*

1   *teaspoon freshly ground black pepper or to taste*

2   *cups rotini pasta*

2   *tablespoons chopped parsley*

1. In a saucepan, cook the chickpeas with enough water to cover until very tender. Hold aside the chickpeas and their cooking liquor.

2. In a saucepan, heat the olive oil and add the rosemary, minced garlic, and chopped anchovy fillets. Cook until the garlic is nicely browned. Add to the chickpeas along with the tomato paste and the water. Season with salt and freshly ground black pepper and bring to a boil.

3. Add the pasta and cook until al dente.

4. Just before serving, stir in the chopped fresh parsley, adjust the seasonings if desired, and serve.

. . . .

Notes and Variations

You can eliminate the anchovies if you are not a fan of anchovies. Rotelle or any pasta can be used in place of the rotini.

. . . .

Lighter Version

Omit the olive oil and salt.
Add an additional teaspoon rosemary and 2 cloves garlic.

NUTRITIONAL ANALYSIS

	Regular		Lighter Version	
Calories:	530		293	
Protein:	14.5	g	14.5	g
Carbohydrates:	51	g	51	g
Dietary Fiber:	7	g	7	g
Fat:	31	g	4	g
Cholesterol:	2.5	mg	2.5	mg
Sodium:	685	mg	152	mg

Percent of Calories

Protein:	11 %		20 %	
Carbohydrates:	38 %		69 %	
Fat:	51 %		12 %	

ROSEMARY AND PARMESAN CHICKPEA TART

Serves 8 as an appetizer

- 1 *pound dried chickpeas, soaked*
- 1 *teaspoon salt*
- 6 *tablespoons fruity olive oil*
- 2 *tablespoons fresh rosemary leaves*
- 1 *teaspoon freshly ground black pepper or to taste*
- 1 *cup grated Parmesan cheese*

. . . .

1. In a saucepan, boil the soaked chickpeas until very tender, but not yet mushy. Drain the chickpeas, reserving the cooking liquor.

2. In a food processor, combine the cooked chickpeas and the salt and process into a thick doughlike mass, adding some of the cooking liquid if necessary. The resulting mass must be dense enough to hold its shape. Place the chickpea mass on a floured surface and mash or roll it out into a circle, about ½ inch thick.

3. Paint the top of the circle with 4 tablespoons olive oil. Sprinkle the tart with the fresh rosemary leaves and season with freshly ground black pepper. Sprinkle the grated Parmesan cheese and remaining 2 tablespoons olive oil over the tart.

4. Bake the chickpea tart in a preheated 375°F oven for 30 minutes, until nicely browned.

5. Cut the chickpea tart into slices and serve hot.

. . . .

Notes and Variations

Other fresh herbs can be used in place of the rosemary such as basil, oregano, or cilantro, or even a combination of fresh herbs. Romano cheese can be used in place of the Parmesan or use both together.

. . . .

Lighter Version

Omit the olive oil and salt. Increase the amount of black pepper by 1 teaspoon and the amount of rosemary by 1 tablespoon. Use ½ cup Parmesan instead of 1 cup.

NUTRITIONAL ANALYSIS

	Regular		Lighter Version	
Calories:	359		245	
Protein:	16	g	14	g
Carbohydrates:	36	g	36	g
Dietary Fiber:	7.5	g	8	g
Fat:	17	g	5.5	g
Cholesterol:	10	mg	5	mg
Sodium:	518	mg	136	mg

Percent of Calories

Protein:	18%		22%	
Carbohydrates:	39%		58%	
Fat:	43%		20%	

TERIYAKI CHICKPEA NUTS   *Serves 8 as an appetizer*

⅓   *cup peanut oil*
1   *pound dried chickpeas, cooked tender, well drained*
6   *tablespoons teriyaki sauce*
2   *teaspoons salt or to taste*

. . . .

1. In a sauté pan, heat the peanut oil and add the cooked chickpeas. Sauté the chickpeas until they begin to color golden.

2. Add the teriyaki sauce and the salt, and shake the sauté pan to coat all the chickpeas evenly. Cover and sauté for about 2 minutes, until all the liquid in the pan is completely absorbed. Adjust salt, if desired.

3. Transfer to a dish and serve hot or at room temperature.

. . . .

Notes and Variations

Walnut or almond oil makes a delicious substitute for the peanut oil. This kind of "nut" appetizer can be done with other beans — red beans, black beans, or soybeans. Simply boil them to a firm-tender stage and proceed as for the chickpeas. They make a great and healthy replacement for peanuts or chips.

Lighter Version

Omit the peanut oil and salt.
Increase the measure of teriyaki sauce
by 2 tablespoons.

NUTRITIONAL ANALYSIS

	Regular		Lighter Version	
Calories:	282		207	
Protein:	11	g	11.5	g
Carbohydrates:	34	g	35	g
Dietary Fiber:	6	g	6	g
Fat:	12	g	3	g
Cholesterol:	0	mg	0	mg
Sodium:	1058	mg	698	mg

Percent of Calories

Protein:	15 %	22 %
Carbohydrates:	47 %	66 %
Fat:	37 %	13 %

TOMATO AND ONION CHICKPEA TART

Serves 8 as an appetizer

1 *pound dried chickpeas, soaked overnight*
2 *teaspoons salt*
4 *large tomatoes, sliced very thin*
2 *large red onions, sliced paper thin*
4 *teaspoons minced fresh oregano leaves*
1 *teaspoon freshly ground black pepper or to taste*
4 *tablespoons fruity olive oil*

1. In a saucepan, simmer the soaked chickpeas until very tender, but not yet mushy. Drain the beans, reserving the cooking liquor.

2. In a food processor, combine the cooked chickpeas and salt and process into a thick doughlike mass, adding some of the cooking liquid if necessary. The resulting mass must be dense enough to hold its shape.

3. Place the chickpea mass on a floured surface and mash or roll it out into a circle, about ½ inch thick. Layer the top of the tart with the thinly sliced tomatoes and red onions. Season with the minced oregano and freshly ground black pepper. Sprinkle on the olive oil.

4. Bake the chickpea tart in a preheated 375°F oven for 30 minutes, until the topping is fairly dry and the edges of the tart are browned.

5. Cut the tomato and onion chickpea tart into slices and serve hot.

Notes and Variations

A julienne of bell peppers and white onions makes another nice topping for this tart. Basil or fresh rosemary leaves can be used in place of the oregano.

Lighter Version

Omit the salt and olive oil. Increase the chopped oregano from 4 teaspoons to 2 tablespoons and the black pepper from 1 teaspoon to 2 teaspoons.

NUTRITIONAL ANALYSIS

	Regular		Lighter Version	
Calories:	283		224	
Protein:	11.5	g	11.5	g
Carbohydrates:	39	g	39	g
Dietary Fiber:	7	g	7	g
Fat:	10	g	3.5	g
Cholesterol:	0	mg	0	mg
Sodium:	550	mg	17	mg

Percent of Calories

Protein:	16 %	20 %
Carbohydrates:	53 %	67 %
Fat:	31 %	13 %

TURKISH CHICKPEA CROQUETTES

Serves 8 as an entree

1 pound dried chickpeas
1 pound finely ground lean lamb
1 large onion, minced
1 cup crumbled feta cheese
½ cup minced parsley
2 tablespoons minced fresh dill
2 teaspoons salt or to taste
1 teaspoon freshly ground black pepper or to taste
4 raw medium eggs, lightly beaten
2 cups all-purpose flour, or more if necessary
1 quart oil, or more, for deep frying

1. Cook the chickpeas until very tender and puree in a food processor, or just mash them in a bowl with a wooden spoon or potato ricer.

2. In a food processor, combine the lamb and chickpeas and process into a "dough." Add the minced onion, crumbled feta, minced parsley and dill, salt, black pepper, and lightly beaten eggs. Process again until well blended.

3. Moisten your hands with water, then take an amount of the mixture equivalent to a medium egg, and mold with your hands into a football shape. Roll the croquettes in flour and transfer to a platter until all the mixture has been made into croquettes.

4. Heat about 1 inch of oil in a frying pan or skillet to 350°F.

5. Carefully lay the croquettes in the heated oil, as many at a time as possible without crowding the pan. Fry for about 7 minutes, turning them over and over until they are golden brown on all sides and cooked completely through.

6. With a slotted spatula transfer the cooked croquettes to a baking pan lined with absorbent paper to drain, and hold in a warm oven. Continue until all the croquettes are done.

7. Serve hot.

. . . .

Notes and Variations

This dish can also be made with ground lean pork or turkey. Parmesan can be used in place of the feta if you want a stronger cheese flavor. Two teaspoons dried dill leaves can be used in place of the 2 tablespoons fresh dill.

. . . .

Lighter Version

In this recipe the croquettes are baked rather than fried, eliminating the frying oil altogether. After rolling the croquettes in flour, transfer to a nonstick baking sheet. Preheat an oven to 400°F. Bake the croquettes for about 20 minutes, until they are golden brown and cooked all the way through. Serve hot. Increase the dill from 2 to 4 tablespoons. Omit the salt. Reduce the feta cheese from 1 to ½ cup. Replace the 4 large raw eggs with 8 large raw egg whites.

NUTRITIONAL ANALYSIS

	Regular		Lighter Version	
Calories:	867		492	
Protein:	39	g	37	g
Carbohydrates:	62.5	g	62	g
Dietary Fiber:	9	g	9	g
Fat:	52	g	10.5	g
Cholesterol:	188	mg	57	mg
Sodium:	1006	mg	210	mg

Percent of Calories

Protein:	18 %	30 %
Carbohydrates:	29 %	51 %
Fat:	53 %	19 %

Lentils

Brown Lentil, Green Lentil, Masur

Lens esculenta
ORIGIN: MIDDLE EAST

Red Lentil, Crimson Lentil

Lens culinaris
ORIGIN: TURKEY

Lentils are one of the earliest cultivated of pulses, as early as 7,000 B.C. They were and are today extremely important to the food supply in Turkey and the Middle East as well as to the Mediterranean area. In France, the world's most prized lentil, a green lentil, is grown in the areas surrounding the town of Lepuy, and the lentils are called Lentilles Lepuy.

The lentil pod is small, containing only two seeds. The color of the seeds, or lentils, vary from dark brown, to green, gray, red, crimson, and yellow. Some seed coats are mottled and speckled.

Lentils are cultivated in North Africa, the Middle East, the Mediterranean coast, and in Europe, including France, Germany, and the Netherlands.

Lentils are eaten as the immature pods as vegetables, and the seeds are dried as a pulse, and sometimes split for faster cooking in soups and stews.

BROWN LENTILS WITH BACON AND BALSAMIC VINEGAR

Serves 6 as a side

1 *pound dried brown lentils*

6 *cups water*

2 *tablespoons balsamic vinegar*

1 *teaspoon dried rosemary leaves*

6 *strips bacon*

1 *medium onion, finely chopped*

1 *teaspoon salt*

¼ *teaspoon black pepper*

1 *teaspoon hot pepper sauce or to taste*

1. Gently simmer the lentils in the water with the balsamic vinegar and rosemary for 45 minutes, until tender.

2. Cook the bacon in a frying pan until crisp.

3. Remove the bacon from the pan and set aside. Add the chopped onion. Brown the onion in the bacon drippings. Add the browned onion and bacon drippings to the lentil pot. Simmer for another 15 minutes.

4. Crumble the crisp bacon and add to the lentils.

5. Season with salt, black pepper, and hot sauce.

6. Serve the lentils hot as a side or chilled as a cold side or salad.

....

Notes and Variations

Use Creole red pickled onions or English-style pickled onions in place of the fresh onion. Lentils lend themselves well to a crisp vinegar taste. This recipe also works well with haricot beans. Simply simmer until they are tender to the bite and proceed from there. Fresh chopped parsley, chervil, or dill before serving is a tasty addition.

....

Lighter Version

Omit the salt. Replace the pork bacon with turkey bacon. Brown the chopped onion in a dry, nonstick pan, stirring constantly to prevent sticking and burning.

NUTRITIONAL ANALYSIS

	Regular		Lighter Version	
Calories:	361		293	
Protein:	23	g	23.5	g
Carbohydrates:	4	g	45	g
Dietary Fiber:	10	g	10	g
Fat:	11	g	3.5	g
Cholesterol:	12.5	mg	10	mg
Sodium:	504	mg	199	mg

Percent of Calories

Protein:	25%	31%
Carbohydrates:	49%	59%
Fat:	26%	10%

CASTILIAN BROWN LENTIL SOUP *Serves 6*

1 cup brown lentils, rinsed

6 cups chicken stock

2 strips bacon, finely chopped

2 bay leaves

1 tablespoon chopped parsley

1½ tablespoons olive oil

1 medium onion, chopped

1 medium carrot, scraped and chopped

2 cloves garlic, chopped

1 large tomato, peeled, seeded, and chopped

2 teaspoons paprika

2 teaspoons salt or to taste

1 teaspoon freshly ground black pepper

1. In a saucepan, combine the brown lentils with the chicken stock, chopped bacon, bay leaves, and parsley. Bring to a boil, cover, and turn down to a gentle simmer.

2. In a sauté pan or skillet, heat the olive oil and sauté the chopped onion and carrot until they begin to color.

3. Add the chopped garlic and tomato and cook together for about 2 minutes. Add the mixture to the lentil pot.

4. Season with paprika, salt, and freshly ground black pepper to taste.

5. Simmer gently for about 1 hour, until the lentils are very tender. Remove the bay leaves.

Notes and Variations

Red lentils can be used here. The chicken stock can be replaced with beef stock. The parsley can be added just before serving rather than in the beginning to give a fresh "green" flavor to the soup. Two chorizo sausages can be sliced into ½-inch rounds to replace the bacon. This is a simple Spanish country soup.

Lighter Version

Omit the bacon, olive oil, and salt. Replace the regular chicken stock with nonfat, low-sodium chicken broth. Add 1 bay leaf, 2 tablespoons parsley, 1 teaspoon paprika, and 1 clove garlic.

NUTRITIONAL ANALYSIS

	Regular		Lighter Version	
Calories:	242		148	
Protein:	15.5	g	11	g
Carbohydrates:	24	g	27	g
Dietary Fiber:	5.5	g	5.5	g
Fat:	10	g	<1	g
Cholesterol:	5.5	mg	0	mg
Sodium:	1550	mg	12	mg

Percent of Calories

Protein:	25 %	28 %
Carbohydrates:	39 %	68 %
Fat:	36 %	4 %

CYPRIAN SOUR LENTIL SOUP

Serves 8

 1 *pound brown lentils, rinsed and picked over*
10 *cups water*
 2 *cups chopped green onions*
 4 *cloves garlic, minced*
 6 *tablespoons minced fresh cilantro*
 4 *tablespoons virgin olive oil*
½ *cup cold water*
 2 *tablespoons flour*
 6 *tablespoons cider vinegar*
 2 *teaspoons salt*
 1 *teaspoon freshly ground black pepper*

1. In a soup pot or large saucepan, combine the brown lentils with the water, chopped green onions, minced garlic, minced cilantro, and olive oil. Bring to a boil. Turn down to a gentle simmer, cover, and cook for 1 hour, until the lentils are very tender.

2. Whisk the water and flour together and stir into the soup along with the cider vinegar. Season to taste with salt and freshly ground black pepper. Continue simmering for another 15 minutes and serve.

Notes and Variations

Red lentils and dried haricot beans can be used in this recipe. If using a haricot bean, presoak and cook according to the correct time for that bean. Chicken or beef stock can replace the water for a richer soup. The cider vinegar can be replaced with red or white wine vinegar, tarragon vinegar, or balsamic vinegar. If the liquid reduces too much in the cooking, add more water or stock.

Lighter Version

Omit the olive oil and salt.
Increase the garlic by 2 cloves.

NUTRITIONAL ANALYSIS

	Regular		Lighter Version	
Calories:	217		170	
Protein:	13.5	g	13	g
Carbohydrates:	29.5	g	30	g
Dietary Fiber:	6.5	g	6.5	g
Fat:	6	g	<1	g
Cholesterol:	0	mg	0	mg
Sodium:	435	mg	8	mg

Percent of Calories

Protein:	24%	30%
Carbohydrates:	53%	67%
Fat:	24%	3%

HOT LENTIL SALAD
WITH ANDOUILLE AND GARLIC

Serves 8

> 3 *cups dried brown lentils*
> 8 *cups water*
> 2 *tablespoons butter*
> 1 *pound andouille sausage, cut crosswise into 1-inch lengths*
> 1 *medium onion, chopped*
> 4 *cloves garlic, minced*
> 6 *tablespoons olive oil*
> 2 *tablespoons red wine vinegar*
> ¼ *cup chopped parsley*
> 1 *teaspoon salt*
> ½ *teaspoon freshly ground black pepper*

1. In a saucepan, combine the lentils with the water. Bring the water to a boil, turn down to a simmer, cover, and cook for 40 minutes, until the lentils are tender.

2. In a separate sauté pan, while the lentils are cooking, heat the butter and brown the andouille sausage pieces with the chopped onion and garlic. Add to the lentils and simmer together for 5 minutes.

3. To complete the hot lentil salad, drain the lentils and transfer to a bowl. Stir in the olive oil, red wine vinegar, and chopped parsley. Season to taste with salt and freshly ground black pepper.

4. Serve hot.

Notes and Variations

Andouille is a highly seasoned, garlicky beef and pork sausage made in Louisiana. It is used in gumbos, jambalayas, and any other dish that calls for a well-flavored sausage. Another smoked sausage can be used in place of the andouille. This salad can also be served at room temperature or even cold.

Lighter Version

Omit the butter, olive oil, and salt. Replace the andouille sausage with a low-fat turkey sausage. Increase the vinegar by 2 tablespoons.

NUTRITIONAL ANALYSIS

	Regular		Lighter Version	
Calories:	544		334	
Protein:	28	g	29.5	g
Carbohydrates:	45	g	45	g
Dietary Fiber:	10	g	10	g
Fat:	29	g	5	g
Cholesterol:	46	mg	35	mg
Sodium:	915	mg	519	mg

Percent of Calories

Protein:	20 %		34 %	
Carbohydrates:	32 %		52 %	
Fat:	47 %		14 %	

HUNGARIAN LENTIL AND CORNISH HEN SOUP

Serves 10

4 *strips bacon, diced*

2 *large Cornish hens*

12 *cups chicken stock*

1 *pound dry brown lentils*

2 *carrots, diced*

2 *turnips, diced*

2 *medium onions, chopped*

2 *stalks celery, chopped*

¼ *cup chopped parsley*

4 *tablespoons butter*

4 *tablespoons flour*

2 *teaspoons salt or to taste*

1 *teaspoon freshly ground black pepper or to taste*

½ *teaspoon dry mustard*

½ *cup heavy cream*

1. In a large saucepan or soup pot, add the diced bacon and the raw Cornish hens. Sauté together until all the fat is rendered from the bacon and the hens are lightly browned on all sides.

2. Add the chicken stock, lentils, diced carrots and turnips, chopped onions, celery, and parsley and bring to a gentle simmer. Cook for 1 ½ hours, until the Cornish hen meat is falling off the bones.

3. Carefully lift the birds from the soup onto a cutting board or plate. Remove the meat from the carcasses and cut into bite-sized pieces. Return it to the soup. Discard the bird carcasses.

4. Make a roux in a small saucepan by melting the butter and blending in the flour. Cook while stirring until the roux becomes golden brown.

Whisk about 1 cup of the soup liquor into the roux and stir the roux into the soup. Season to taste with salt and freshly ground black pepper. Continue simmering for 15 minutes.

5. Just before serving, blend in the dry mustard and heavy cream.

. . . .

Notes and Variations

This traditional Hungarian soup was originally conceived with partridge in place of the Cornish hens. I use Cornish hens or chicken because they are more easily available and far less costly. This soup also works nicely with veal — use 1 to 1½ pounds.

. . . .

Lighter Version

Omit the butter, salt, and heavy cream. Replace the bacon with low-fat, turkey bacon. Replace the regular chicken stock with nonfat, low-sodium chicken broth. Increase the parsley measure by ¼ cup and the dry mustard by 1 teaspoon.

NUTRITIONAL ANALYSIS

	Regular		Lighter Version	
Calories:	430		299	
Protein:	29	g	24.5	g
Carbohydrates:	35	g	37.5	g
Dietary Fiber:	7.5	g	7.5	g
Fat:	19.5	g	6.5	g
Cholesterol:	60.5	mg	31	mg
Sodium:	1591	mg	203	mg

Percent of Calories

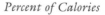

Protein:	27%	32%
Carbohydrates:	32%	49%
Fat:	41%	19%

IRANIAN LENTIL PASTRIES

Serves 6 as an appetizer or side

Makes about 24 pastries

¾ cup dried brown lentils

2¼ cups water

1 packet double-acting yeast

¾ cup warm water

2 teaspoons rose water

2 cups presifted all-purpose flour

1 teaspoon salt

½ teaspoon ground cardamom

3 tablespoons softened butter, plus 3 tablespoons butter

2 medium onions, chopped

1 teaspoon salt or to taste

1½ tablespoons brown sugar

Peanut oil for deep frying

. . . .

1. While the dough is rising, rinse and pick over the lentils and transfer them to a saucepan with the water. Bring the water to a boil, cover, turn down to a gentle simmer, and cook for an hour or so, until the lentils are very tender and the liquid is almost completely reduced. Transfer the softened lentils to a bowl and mash with a fork or puree them in a food processor.

2. In a bowl, sprinkle the yeast over the warm water and stir to dissolve. Add the rose water.

3. Work in the flour, ½ cup at a time, as well as the salt, cardamom and softened butter, until you have a dough. Transfer to a floured surface and knead for 10 minutes, until the dough is smooth and elastic. Cover the dough with a damp cloth and allow to rise for about 1 hour, until the dough has doubled in bulk.

4. In a sauté pan, heat the 3 tablespoons remaining butter and sauté the chopped onions until they begin to color. Add the lentils and season to taste with salt. Add the brown sugar. Cook together for another 5 minutes, remove from the heat, and allow to cool.

5. Uncover the risen dough and punch it down. Roll out the dough on a floured surface into a large thin rectangle about 13 by 19 inches. Cut the dough into 3-inch rounds.

6. Place a rounded teaspoon of the lentil mixture in the center of each round. Moisten the edges of the rounds with water and fold the dough over to form half circles, pinching the edges together to seal. Arrange the pastries on a platter until they are all made.

7. In a frying pan or skillet, heat a 1-inch depth of oil to 375°F. Slide the pastries into the oil, as many as you can, without crowding the pan. Fry the pastries for 2 minutes on one side and 1 minute on the other. Using a slotted spoon or spatula, transfer the lentil pastries to a platter lined with absorbent paper to drain and serve immediately.

Notes and Variations

These pastries are not light sweet desserts. They are substantial in texture and serve as a bread with a meal or alone as a snack — and in some cases a meal in itself. Red lentils can be used in this dish as well as any dried haricot bean. Cook the haricots until soft and proceed from there. More salt can be sprinkled over the pastries before serving, if you like, or even a sprinkle of freshly squeezed lemon juice. You can also serve the pastries with a dipping sauce such as hummus or garlic tahini.

. . . .

Lighter Version

Omit the salt and butter in both the dough and the lentils. Cook the onions in a nonstick pan until they begin to color. Stir them around in the pan constantly while cooking so they don't burn. Don't fry the pastries in oil. Arrange on a nonstick baking sheet and bake in a preheated 375°F oven for 12 to 15 minutes, until they are puffed and golden brown. Sprinkle 2 tablespoons of lemon juice over the lentil pastries before serving.

NUTRITIONAL ANALYSIS

	Regular		Lighter Version	
Calories:	481		221	
Protein:	9.5	g	9.5	g
Carbohydrates:	45	g	45	g
Dietary Fiber:	4	g	4	g
Fat:	30.1	g	<1	g
Cholesterol:	31	mg	0	mg
Sodium:	833	mg	5	mg

Percent of Calories

Protein:	8%	17%
Carbohydrates:	36%	81%
Fat:	56%	3%

LENTIL PUREE

Serves 8

   1   *pound dried brown lentils*
   8   *cups water*
   4   *bay leaves*
  ¼   *teaspoon ground cloves*
   1   *large chopped onion*
   2   *carrots, chopped*
   4   *cloves garlic, crushed*
   1   *large stalk celery, stringed and chopped*
  ½   *teaspoon dried thyme*
   4   *tablespoons butter*
  ¼   *cup chopped parsley*
   1   *teaspoon salt or to taste*
  ½   *teaspoon freshly ground black pepper or to taste*

1. In a saucepan, combine the lentils with the water, bay leaves, and ground cloves and bring to a boil. Turn down to a simmer, cover, and cook for 25 minutes.

2. Add the chopped onion, carrots, crushed garlic, chopped celery, and thyme. Bring to a boil again, turn down to a simmer, cover and cook for 15 minutes more, until the lentils are very tender. Drain the lentils, reserving the cooking liquor. Discard the bay leaves.

3. Transfer the lentils to a blender or food processor container. Process into a puree using some of the lentil cooking liquor if necessary.

4. In a saucepan, heat the butter until it just begins to color. Add the lentil puree and sauté until the puree is thick enough to hold its own shape.

5. Fold in the chopped parsley, season to taste with salt and freshly ground black pepper, and serve.

· ·

Notes and Variations

Brown or red lentils can be used here, as well as any cooked haricot bean. Allspice or nutmeg can replace the ground cloves. The thyme can be replaced with oregano and the parsley can be replaced with 2 tablespoons fresh basil or cilantro. Olive oil will render a fruitier flavor, while the cooked butter renders a nutty flavor. Heavy cream in place of the cooking liquor, added while pureeing the cooked lentils, will make a richer dish.

· ·

Lighter Version

Omit the butter and salt. Increase the ground cloves by ¼ teaspoon, the crushed garlic cloves by 2, and the black pepper by ½ teaspoon. After pureeing the cooked lentils, return to a saucepan and heat to dry them out enough to hold their own shape; stir constantly so they don't stick and burn.

NUTRITIONAL ANALYSIS

	Regular		Lighter Version	
Calories:	257		208	
Protein:	16.5	g	16.5	g
Carbohydrates:	35.5	g	36	g
Dietary Fiber:	8.5	g	8.5	g
Fat:	6.5	g	<1	g
Cholesterol:	15.5	mg	0	mg
Sodium:	343	mg	18	mg

Percent of Calories

Protein:	25%	30%
Carbohydrates:	54%	67%
Fat:	22%	3%

SYRIAN LENTIL-STUFFED CABBAGE ROLLS

Serves 8 as an entree

6 tablespoons light-flavored olive oil, plus ½ cup
8 green onions, chopped
1½ cups cooked white rice
4 cups cooked brown lentils
2 large tomatoes, skinned, seeded, and chopped
½ cup minced parsley
¼ cup minced fresh cilantro
½ teaspoon ground allspice
½ teaspoon cumin
3 teaspoons salt or to taste
1 teaspoon freshly ground black pepper
  Water
32 large raw cabbage leaves
8 cloves garlic, pressed
¾ cup freshly squeezed lemon juice

1. In a sauté pan or skillet, heat 6 tablespoons olive oil and sauté the chopped green onions until limp.

2. Transfer the cooked green onions to a bowl and add the cooked rice, cooked brown lentils, chopped tomatoes, minced parsley, minced cilantro, allspice, cumin, and season with 2 teaspoons salt and freshly ground black pepper. Set aside.

3. In a soup pot, bring enough water to cover the raw cabbage leaves to a boil. Blanch the cabbage leaves in the boiling water until they are pliable. Carefully remove the now tender leaves to drain and cool. When the leaves are cool enough to handle, lay them out one by one and cut out the remaining stiff middle ribs of each. Arrange these removed ribs to line the fireproof-covered baking dish or casserole that you will use to cook the cabbage rolls.

4. Take the trimmed cabbage leaves and in the center of each place a rounded tablespoon of the lentil and rice stuffing. Roll up the leaves

as you go, folding in the sides first to keep in the filling. Arrange the cabbage rolls in the baking dish.

5. In a small bowl, combine the pressed garlic with the 1 teaspoon salt, lemon juice, and ½ cup olive oil. Pour the mixture over the cabbage rolls in the baking dish. Add water, just enough to barely cover the cabbage rolls. Cover the baking dish with foil. Place the baking dish on the stove top and bring to a very gentle simmer. Simmer for about 45 minutes. Remove from the heat and allow to cool to lukewarm in the pan liquid.

6. Serve lukewarm or at room temperature.

· ·

Notes and Variations

Red lentils or any cooked dried haricot all work well in this recipe. Brown rice or Arborio rice can replace the white rice. These cabbage rolls are delicious served hot with a cornstarch-thickened reduction of the pan liquid as sauce.

· ·

Lighter Version

Omit the olive oil and salt throughout. Increase the measure of cumin by ½ teaspoon.

NUTRITIONAL ANALYSIS

	Regular		Lighter Version	
Calories:	392		244	
Protein:	14.5	g	14.5	g
Carbohydrates:	48	g	48	g
Dietary Fiber:	11.5	g	11.5	g
Fat:	18.5	g	1.5	g
Cholesterol:	0	mg	0	mg
Sodium:	856	mg	57	mg

Percent of Calories		
Protein:	14 %	22 %
Carbohydrates:	46 %	72 %
Fat:	40 %	6 %

ARMENIAN RED LENTIL SOUP   *Serves 6*

6 cups lamb stock (traditional) or other stock
1 cup red lentils, rinsed
2 tablespoons butter
2 large onions, chopped
2 teaspoons salt or to taste
1 teaspoon freshly ground black pepper or to taste
1 teaspoon hot Hungarian paprika or to taste

. . . .

1. Bring the stock to a boil in a saucepan. Add the rinsed red lentils, cover, and simmer gently for 45 minutes.

2. Heat the butter in a sauté pan and sauté the chopped onions until browned lightly. Add the cooked onions to the lentil pan.

3. Season to taste with salt, freshly ground black pepper, and paprika. Simmer for 15 minutes more, until the lentils are very tender.

. . . .

Notes and Variations

The lamb stock can be replaced with beef, veal, or chicken stock. The paprika is important in this recipe. Do your best to find a good quality robust-flavored paprika and not just a light-flavored paprika that adds more color than flavor. Brown lentils work equally as well as red in this soup.

. . . .

Lighter Version

Whether you use lamb, beef, veal, or chicken stock or broth, be sure that it is nonfat, low sodium. Omit the butter and salt. Add 1 more teaspoon paprika, or 2 if you like it spicy.

NUTRITIONAL ANALYSIS

	Regular		Lighter Version	
Calories:	175		142	
Protein:	12.5	g	14	g
Carbohydrates:	22	g	22	g
Dietary Fiber:	5	g	5	g
Fat:	5	g	<1	g
Cholesterol:	10.5	mg	0	mg
Sodium:	1536	mg	74	mg

Percent of Calories

Protein:	27%	38%
Carbohydrates:	49%	59%
Fat:	24%	3%

EGYPTIAN RED LENTIL SOUP

Serves 10

1 *pound red lentils*
2½ *quarts chicken stock*
1 *large onion, pureed*
1 *teaspoon ground cumin*
2 *teaspoons salt or to taste*
1 *teaspoon freshly ground black pepper or to taste*
2 *tablespoons lemon juice*
Egyptian Onion Sauce (optional) (page 349)

1. Rinse and pick over the red lentils.

2. In a soup pot or saucepan, bring the chicken stock to a boil and add the lentils and onion. Return to the boil and turn down to a gentle simmer. Cover and cook for approximately 1 hour, until the lentils have practically cooked into a puree.

3. Add the ground cumin and season to taste with salt and freshly ground black pepper.

4. To serve, stir in the lemon juice and ladle the soup into bowls. Garnish each serving with a dollop of Egyptian onion sauce.

Notes and Variations

This is an extremely simple and satisfying soup. Either brown or red lentils can be used here. The chicken stock can be replaced by fish, veal, or beef stock, depending on which flavor direction you want the soup to follow. The cumin can be replaced by curry. If the soup becomes too thick in the cooking, add water or more stock.

Lighter Version

Replace the chicken stock with nonfat, low-sodium chicken broth. Increase the cumin by ½ teaspoon and the lemon juice by 2 tablespoons.

NUTRITIONAL ANALYSIS

	Regular		Lighter Version	
Calories:	183		177	
Protein:	14.5	g	14	g
Carbohydrates:	29	g	31	g
Dietary Fiber:	6.5	g	6.5	g
Fat:	1.5	g	<1	g
Cholesterol:	0	mg	0	mg
Sodium:	1915	mg	5	mg

Percent of Calories

Protein:	30%		30%	
Carbohydrates:	62%		67%	
Fat:	8%		3%	

HOT RED LENTIL SALAD WITH SALT PORK AND CILANTRO

Serves 8

3   *cups dried lentils*

8   *cups water*

4   *tablespoons olive oil*

8   *ounces salt pork, cut into elongated dice*

2   *tablespoons cider vinegar*

3   *tablespoons chopped cilantro*

1   *teaspoon chili powder*

1   *teaspoon salt or to taste*

½   *teaspoon freshly ground black pepper*

1. In a saucepan, combine the lentils with the water. Bring the water to a boil, turn down to a simmer, cover, and cook for 40 minutes, until the lentils are tender.

2. In a separate sauté pan, heat 2 tablespoons olive oil and sauté the salt pork until most of the fat is rendered. Add the salt pork, fat, and oil in the pan to the lentils and simmer together, until the pan liquid is mostly absorbed or reduced.

3. Transfer the lentils to a heatproof bowl. Stir in the remaining olive oil, cider vinegar, and chopped cilantro. Season with chili powder, salt, and freshly ground black pepper.

4. Serve hot.

Notes and Variations

Other seasoning meats can be used in place of the salt pork such as smoked ham or a nice
sausage cut into thin rounds. A more interesting vinegar such as tarragon or raspberry is
a good replacement for the cider vinegar. Fresh basil or a half-and-half mixture of oregano
and spearmint can replace the cilantro.

Lighter Version

*Omit the olive oil and salt. The salt pork
can be replaced with any low-fat pork
ham or turkey ham. Simply dice it and
add to the lentils after they are cooked.
Add an additional tablespoon each
of cider vinegar and chopped cilantro,
an additional 2 teaspoons chili powder,
and an additional teaspoon pepper.*

NUTRITIONAL ANALYSIS

	Regular		Lighter Version	
Calories:	381		280	
Protein:	23	g	25.5	g
Carbohydrates:	42	g	42.5	g
Dietary Fiber:	9.5	g	10	g
Fat:	14.5	g	2	g
Cholesterol:	14	mg	20	mg
Sodium:	477	mg	337	mg

Percent of Calories

Protein:	23%		35%	
Carbohydrates:	43%		59%	
Fat:	34%		6%	

KUWAIT RED LENTIL SOUP

Serves 10

1 *pound dried red lentils, rinsed and picked over*

12 *cups water*

6 *tablespoons butter*

2 *large onions, finely chopped*

12 *cloves garlic, pressed*

2 *large tomatoes, peeled, seeded, and chopped*

1 *teaspoon ground cardamom*

½ *teaspoon black pepper*

½ *teaspoon ground coriander*

½ *teaspoon ground clove*

½ *teaspoon ground cumin*

½ *teaspoon ground nutmeg*

½ *teaspoon hot paprika*

3 *tablespoons lime juice*

2 *teaspoons salt*

1½ *cups crushed dry vermicelli pasta*

1. In a soup pot or large saucepan, combine the red lentils with the water. Bring to a boil, cover, and turn down to a simmer.

2. In a sauté pan, melt the butter and sauté the chopped onions until translucent. Add the pressed garlic, chopped tomatoes and season with the cardamom, black pepper, coriander, clove, cumin, nutmeg, and paprika. Heat together for 2 minutes and add to the lentil pot along with the lime juice. Simmer for about 45 minutes, until the red lentils are very tender.

3. Season the soup with salt and add the broken vermicelli, adding more water if necessary. Continue simmering until the vermicelli is cooked, about 12 minutes, and serve.

Notes and Variations

Brown lentils or any dried haricot can be used in place of the red lentils. If using a dried haricot, adjust the simmering time accordingly. Any pasta of your preference can be used in place of the vermicelli. A stock, chicken or beef, can be used in place of the water to enrich the flavor of this soup.

Lighter Version

Omit the butter and salt. Increase the hot paprika by 1 ½ teaspoons and the lime juice by 1 tablespoon.

NUTRITIONAL ANALYSIS

	Regular	Lighter Version
Calories:	299	239
Protein:	15.5 g	15.5 g
Carbohydrates:	43.5 g	44 g
Dietary Fiber:	7.5 g	7.5 g
Fat:	8 g	1 g
Cholesterol:	18.5 mg	0 mg
Sodium:	506 mg	9 mg

Percent of Calories

	Regular	Lighter Version
Protein:	20 %	25 %
Carbohydrates:	56 %	71 %
Fat:	23 %	4 %

RED LENTIL SALAD WITH SWEET RED BELL PEPPER AND BALSAMIC VINEGAR

Serves 8

1 *pound red lentils*

8 *cups water*

½ *cup olive oil*

¼ *cup balsamic vinegar*

1 *medium yellow onion, finely chopped*

2 *cloves garlic, minced*

1 *medium sweet red bell pepper, seeded and finely chopped*

¼ *cup chopped parsley*

1 *teaspoon salt*

½ *teaspoon freshly ground black pepper*

1. In a saucepan, combine the lentils with the water. Bring to a boil, turn down to a simmer, and cover. Cook for 35 minutes, until the lentils are cooked tender but not overly so. They should retain some firmness. Drain and allow to cool to room temperature.

2. In a bowl, combine the cooked lentils with the olive oil, balsamic vinegar, chopped onion, garlic, chopped red bell pepper, and chopped parsley. Season to taste with salt and freshly ground black pepper and allow to stand at room temperature for 1 hour before serving to allow the flavors to meld.

Notes and Variations

Red onion or Vidalia onion is good here in place of the yellow onion. The bell pepper can be any color: red, yellow, purple, green, or a mix of colors. Another fresh herb can be used in place of the parsley: basil, oregano. Brown lentils can be used here instead of the red.

Lighter Version

Omit the olive oil and salt. Increase the balsamic vinegar by 2 tablespoons and the pepper by ½ teaspoon.

NUTRITIONAL ANALYSIS

	Regular		Lighter Version	
Calories:	328		212	
Protein:	16.5	g	16.5	g
Carbohydrates:	36	g	37	g
Dietary Fiber:	8	g	8	g
Fat:	14	g	< 1	g
Cholesterol:	0	mg	0	mg
Sodium:	276	mg	10	mg

Percent of Calories

Protein:	19 %	30 %
Carbohydrates:	43 %	68 %
Fat:	38 %	3 %

Sauces

HAZELNUT SAUCE

Serves 6

½ cup shelled hazelnuts

1 cup water or enough to cover the hazelnuts, plus 1 tablespoon water

½ dry cup bread crumbs

2 cloves garlic, chopped

½ cup lightly flavored olive oil

¼ cup distilled white vinegar

1 teaspoon salt or to taste

1. Put the hazelnuts in a heatproof bowl. Bring the 1 cup water to a boil and pour it over the nuts. Allow the hazelnuts to soak in the hot water for several minutes, or long enough to soften their skins. Remove and discard their skins.

2. In a food processor or blender, process the hazelnuts into a coarse paste. Add the bread crumbs, garlic, 1 tablespoon water, and process together. Continue processing as you add the olive oil in a thin stream. Continue processing as you add the vinegar in a thin stream. Season with salt.

3. Store in a tightly capped jar in the refrigerator until ready for use.

. . . .

Notes and Variations

Pecans, walnuts, and cashews all make a good sauce when replacing the hazelnuts. Other oils can replace the olive oil, such as peanut or corn oil. Serve with all kinds of vegetables.

. . . .

Lighter Version

Omit the salt. Replace the olive oil with non-fat yogurt.

NUTRITIONAL ANALYSIS

	Regular		Lighter Version	
Calories:	243		95	
Protein:	2	g	3	g
Carbohydrates:	4.5	g	6	g
Dietary Fiber:	1	g	<1	g
Fat:	25	g	7	g
Cholesterol:	<1	mg	<1	mg
Sodium:	375	mg	35	mg

Percent of Calories

Protein:	3 %		12 %	
Carbohydrates:	7 %		24 %	
Fat:	90 %		64 %	

GARLIC TAHINI SAUCE

Makes 2 cups

  1 cup tahini
  2 large garlic cloves, pressed
  1 tablespoon cider vinegar
  ½ teaspoon salt or to taste
  2 tablespoons freshly squeezed lemon juice
  ½ cup water
  ½ cup chopped parsley
  ½ teaspoon ground cumin

. . . .

1. Combine the tahini in a mixing bowl with the pressed garlic, cider vinegar, and salt. Whisk together.

2. Whisk in the lemon juice, then the water, 1 tablespoon at a time, until the sauce becomes a nice light consistency.

3. Fold in the minced parsley and ground cumin. Adjust the salt and lemon juice to suit your taste.

4. Cover the bowl or transfer to a capped jar and refrigerate until ready for use.

NUTRITIONAL ANALYSIS

Per 1 ounce (2 tablespoons) serving

Calories:	93	
Protein:	3	g
Carbohydrates:	3	g
Dietary Fiber:	1.5	g
Fat:	8.5	g
Cholesterol:	0	g
Sodium:	68	mg

Percent of Calories

Protein:	11%
Carbohydrates:	13%
Fat:	76%

LEMON-GARLIC TAHINI

Serves 8

¾ cup tahini
4 cloves garlic, chopped
1 teaspoon salt or to taste
¾ cup cold water
¾ cup lemon juice

1. In a blender, combine the tahini with the chopped garlic and salt. Process briefly.

2. Combine the cold water and lemon juice. Turn on the blender to high and pour the water-lemon juice mixture into the tahini mixture in a slow, steady stream.

3. Adjust the salt if desired.

4. Store in a tightly capped jar in the refrigerator.

Notes and Variations

You can make this sauce using a small onion in place of the garlic for lemon-onion tahini or use lime instead of lemon for lime-garlic tahini.

. . . .

Lighter Version

There is little one can do to improve the healthful benefits of this sauce other than to omit the salt, which will lower the sodium content to 1.5 mg.

NUTRITIONAL ANALYSIS

Regular

Calories:	144	
Protein:	4	g
Carbohydrates:	6.5	g
Dietary Fiber:	2	g
Fat:	13	g
Cholesterol:	0	mg
Sodium:	268	mg

Percent of Calories

Protein:	11 %
Carbohydrates:	17 %
Fat:	73 %

Egyptian Onion Sauce

Serves 8

> 2 *large onions*
> 4 *tablespoons olive oil*
> 4 *cloves garlic, pressed*
> ¾ *teaspoon salt or to taste*

. . . .

1. Skin the onions and slice paper thin.

2. In a sauté pan, heat the olive oil and sauté the onion slices and pressed garlic until lightly browned.

3. Season with salt and serve hot or at room temperature.

. . . .

Notes and Variations

Onion sauce is generally served as an accompaniment to Middle East dishes, but can be used to improve any dish. Red or Vidalia onions make a sweeter version of the sauce, more of a relish than a sauce. Add 2 teaspoons fresh lemon juice or cider vinegar to give the sauce a bite.

. . . .

Lighter Version

Omit the olive oil and the salt.
Increase the garlic by 2 cloves.
Add 1 tablespoon cider vinegar.

NUTRITIONAL ANALYSIS

	Regular		Lighter Version	
Calories:	76		18	
Protein:	.5	g	.5	g
Carbohydrates:	4	g	4	g
Dietary Fiber:	.5	g	.5	g
Fat:	7	g	<1	g
Cholesterol:	0	mg	0	mg
Sodium:	201	mg	2	mg

Percent of Calories

	Regular	Lighter Version
Protein:	3%	12%
Carbohydrates:	19%	85%
Fat:	78%	3%

Index